P9-DEY-669

THE ART OF BASKETBALL

BY OSCAR ROBERTSON

WITH MICHAEL O'DANIEL

A guide to self-improvement
in the fundamentals of the game

Published by Oscar Robertson Media Ventures

Sale of this book without a front cover may be unauthorized.
If this book is coverless, it may have been reported to the publisher
as "unsold or destroyed" and neither the author nor the publisher
may have received payment for it.

Copyright © 1998 by Oscar Robertson Media Ventures.

All rights reserved, including the right to reproduce this book
or portions thereof in any form whatsoever, except for brief
excerpts in conjunction with book reviews. For information
contact the publisher.

Library of Congress Catalog Card Number: 98-84041

ISBN: 0-9662483-0-9 $12.95

First edition: February 1998

10 9 8 7 6 5 4 3 2 1

Printed in Cincinnati, Ohio by The C.J. Krehbiel Company.

Cover photograph of Oscar Robertson and Lou Hudson:
  James Drake for Sports Illustrated © Time Inc.

Back cover photographs:
  Oscar Robertson and Jerry West © 1998 Wen Roberts / NBA Photos.
  Beverly Hills High School basketball players by Aaron Feldman.

All inside photographs by Aaron Feldman unless otherwise credited.

Cover design: Michael O'Daniel / Paul Feldman

Electronic imaging and prepress: Paul Feldman, Doug Mlyn

Special thanks to Brian McIntyre, National Basketball Association;
  Steve Moeller, University of Cincinnati; David Goldberg,
  Kevin Brown and Beverly Hills High School basketball players.

A publication of Oscar Robertson Media Ventures,
111 N. Beachwood Drive, Los Angeles CA 90004.
US and Canada call toll-free 888-327-1401.
All other countries call 1-213-957-1830 or fax 1-213-957-5114.

Visit our World Wide Web site at http://www.thebigo.com.

**Attention Coaches, Teachers, Camp Directors, Schools,
Boys and Girls Clubs, other nonprofit organizations:**
Discounts are available on purchases of 20 or more copies of
THE ART OF BASKETBALL for educational or fund-raising uses.
For more information, please write, call or e-mail the publisher.

Additional order forms and information opposite page 96.

A portion of the proceeds from the sale of this book will go
to the National Kidney Foundation.

THE ART OF BASKETBALL

CONTENTS

DEDICATION

This book is dedicated first to my older brothers Bailey and Henry Robertson, who encouraged and inspired me both on and off the court.

It is also dedicated to my first coach, Tom Sleet, who took an interest in me when I was a rawboned kid with no formal knowledge of the game and got me started on the road to success. Working with a group of inner-city kids who took life one day at a time and had no dreams for the future, he molded us into good citizens and gave us self-confidence, a winning attitude and the encouragement to succeed on the court and in all other facets of life.

Next, a special thank you to my high school coaches, Ray Crowe and Al Spurlock, who helped me build on the foundation Tom Sleet had constructed. Through their teaching and knowledge of the game, these men created a tradition of excellence and teamwork at Crispus Attucks High School that I feel will never be duplicated anywhere else.

Finally, I dedicate this book to all aspiring players everywhere, male and female, young and not as young, all over the world. I hope you get the same enjoyment out of becoming a better basketball player that I did. I firmly believe that the harder you work to improve your skills, the more you'll enjoy the process. Even if you never play in organized competition, take pride in the fact that you took up the challenge to make a better player of yourself. It will serve you well in life.

—OSCAR ROBERTSON

This photo from a game against the Celtics illustrates some of the techniques we'll cover in this book: how to get the ball out of a jam and upcourt quickly following a rebound; protecting the ball with your body when you dribble; dribbling with your left hand because here it's farther from the defensive player; keeping the ball low for better control; dribbling with your fingertips; keeping your head up and the entire court in focus so you can see how the play is developing; using a good first step to accelerate past a defender. These are things you'll learn to do instinctively in a split second; they're based more on common sense than anything else. Practice according to the guidelines in this book and you'll see how all these techniques go into making you a more complete player.

© 1998 Ken Regan / NBA Photos

INTRODUCTION

I call this book THE ART OF BASKETBALL because I believe basketball *is* an art. When the game is played as it should be played, you'll see athletes who perform with precision, finesse, rhythm, flair and grace. Watch a game with the sound off sometime and you'll see what I mean.

A dancer will practice the same steps, a violinist the same scales, an athlete the same motions, over and over. Is the athlete not also an artist? We all strive to become as good as we can; we practice long hours voluntarily because we love what we do. Some become virtuoso performers, some are happy with a place in the ensemble, but the path to fulfillment is the same for us all.

In 1964, I brought out an instructional book called PLAY BETTER BASKETBALL, devoted solely to the fundamentals of the game: dribbling, passing, shooting, rebounding, defense and conditioning. I saw a need for such a book because so many of the coaches' and athletes' books on the market at that time either focused almost completely on strategy, or took a fairly superficial approach to fundamentals.

Our book offered detailed instruction on the most basic aspects of the game, so that players of any age could develop fundamental skills through practice on their own, much as I had done. One of the things I've always loved about basketball is that you *can* develop many of the skills on your own.

Basketball has expanded considerably since that book was published. (As has the number of basketball books on the market). The National Basketball Association now has 29 teams instead of eight; there are some 200 professional leagues throughout the world; and best of all, women now have an equal opportunity to play at every level including professionally (although not yet for equal money). And there have been changes in the rules at the high school, college and professional levels.

What has not changed is the need for players to excel in the fundamentals of the game. Much of the *emphasis* has changed to flash and muscle instead of good basic basketball. Looking at the way the game is played today, I see even more of a need for a return to emphasis on the fundamentals.

A PLAN FOR SELF-IMPROVEMENT

THE ART OF BASKETBALL goes into even more depth on fundamentals than my first book, and guides you to self-improvement through practice. It's important to plan, set goals, practice intelligently and measure your progress. This is how an artist works. A concert pianist usually doesn't sit down and play a new piece from scratch. He or she isolates certain passages—some for the right hand, some for the left, some for both—and masters each individual passage before putting everything together.

A true artist also develops an individual style, a conceptual approach to his or her art. I feel you can develop a conceptual approach to basketball. Start with being a two-handed basketball player. That in itself puts you far ahead of everyone else. If you master the fundamentals, there will always be a place for you on the court, even if you play with people who may have more athletic ability.

I was fortunate to grow up in Indianapolis, an environment where people took basketball seriously. At an early age, I saw that if I wanted to play with older, more experienced players, I'd have to practice on my own to bring my skills up to their level. They weren't running a clinic, and they weren't about to let anybody on the court who would slow them down.

That was my first lesson: The best way to improve is to play with people who are better than you are. I played against some *great* players, and developed my game in response to what they were did. For example, I got tired of getting my jump shot blocked and had to figure out a way to get the shot off against taller and stronger players. I never thought I was that special; the minute you got the idea you were best in your class, someone else would come along and "take you to school."

WHY YOU HAVE TO PRACTICE ON YOUR OWN

Lesson number two was that you had homework in basketball just as you did in school. I gave myself a daily assignment: layups and tip-ins with either hand, free throws, crossover dribbles, reverse pivots, dribbling with my left hand. I worked on shooting from spots where I had difficulty: bank shots from every conceivable angle, side shots, hook shots, shots moving to the basket. Then I couldn't wait to get into a game and try them out. If something didn't work, it was back to the woodshed. When something did work, how could I use it to better advantage? This was fun!

Suppose you're part of a team and you already practice two hours a day. Why is it necessary for you to practice on your own? Here's why. Your coach is concerned with (1) whatever it takes for your team to win (that's how he or she keeps the job), (2) your individual development as a player to the extent it affects the team. The coach may or may not have the time or the inclination to work with you individually. You're responsible for filling in the gaps in your game. That's reality.

LEARNING TO THINK LIKE A WINNER

While constant repetition helped me develop "muscle memory," I saw that athletic skill by itself would not be enough. Why could some people always perform and others were inconsistent?

Lesson number three was the importance of your mental approach to the game, something I came to appreciate more the longer I played. For example, the single biggest factor in improving your game is your determination to improve. That's mental. Sticking to a regular practice schedule is mental. Learning from your mistakes, developing your concentration, playing with intensity, using common sense, building your confidence—all these are part of your mental approach to the game.

If you've got both the physical *and* the mental skills, you've put the complete package together. Right? Wrong. You're still just one person. You have to surround yourself with others who take the game as seriously as you do, who know how to win, who will do what it takes to win.

Lesson number four: Talent is important, but results are more important. What does it take to produce results as a team? Focus your game on doing that. A fundamentally sound, team-oriented player will take pride in his or her defense, rebounding, passing, blocking out under the boards, setting picks, moving without the ball—things that contribute to the good of the team—and take special pride in being able to execute in critical situations.

YOU'RE IN CONTROL

The final step is the transition from knowledge to performance. You know what you have to do; now you must play with confidence, aggressiveness and control. *Confidence:* You're fearless. You firmly believe in yourself and will not allow that belief to be shaken. *Aggressiveness:* You seize the initiative, dictate the terms of the game, stay on the attack. *Control* means not merely command of the situation, but control of yourself. You play with intensity and passion but let reason prevail; you keep your emotions under control. You refuse to get rattled, no matter how hard anyone tries. You're focused totally on winning. You're satisfied *only* when the team wins; individual statistics are immaterial. You know there's always room for improvement, both individually and as a team.

IDEAL PLAYER PROFILES

When a company has job openings to fill, its personnel department often creates "ideal candidate profiles" describing the qualifications it expects of the applicants who hope to fill those positions. To give you a model to shoot for, I thought it would be interesting to create Ideal Player Profiles, first of a complete all-around player, and then for each individual position.

THE IDEAL ALL-AROUND PLAYER

Whatever his or her position, this player will have command of the fundamentals of the game, and specifically should be able to dribble with either hand, shoot layups and tip-ins with either hand, execute a crossover dribble, a reverse pivot, a pick and roll, set picks, block out under the boards, and handle the ball against the press. The major physical and mental attributes I'd look for include:

Quickness	Concentration	Will power
Strength	Intensity	Control
Flexibility	Common sense	Commitment
Endurance	Confidence	Awareness
Peripheral Vision	Courage	Adaptability
Pride	Reliability	Strong work ethic

Height and speed are desirable, of course, but preferably in combination with the qualities above.

IDEAL PLAYERS AT EACH POSITION

CENTERS

Good defensively
Able to tip if in position
Sets picks
Great rebounder
Can shoot the hook shot
  with either hand
Helps teammates on defense
Can pass in tight situations
Accurate shot in close
  and up to 15 feet out
Blocks off the boards
Best at the pick & roll
Has good mobility,
  is not stationary
Able to play facing
  away from basket
Good speed up and
  down the court
Agile enough to block
  or deny shots

FORWARDS

Good defensively
Better rebounder
Playmaker
Able to penetrate
Good speed up and
  down the court
Good shot from corner
Able to shoot coming
  off screens
Moves well without
  the ball
Able to go left or right
Able to pass to pivot
  in all situations
Sets picks
Follows his/her shots
Good judgement as to
  when/when not to
  pass or shoot
Able to shoot moving
  toward the basket
Blocks off the boards

GUARDS

Good dribbler
Doesn't dribble excessively
Always keeps head up,
  has court fully in view
Accurate shot from 15–18 feet
Able to pass on the run
Able to pass off the dribble
Able to initiate the fast break
Able to control the game
Commands the respect
  of his/her teammates
Outstanding defensively
Protects against fast break,
  doesn't get caught under
  offensive basket
Aggressive, able to penetrate
Able to execute pick & roll
Willing to go to the basket
  often enough to keep
  the defense off balance

You can see what you have to do. It isn't anywhere nearly as overwhelming as it appears. These are all skills the average player can and should develop, and some are just plain common sense.

BASIC RULES AND TERMS

If you're not already familiar with the rules of basketball, you should be able to get a rule book at a sporting goods store, or visit the website for FIBA (International Basketball Federation) at http://www.fiba.com, for the complete international rulebook, or the USA Basketball website at http://www.usabasketball.com for a synopsis of U.S. and international rules. The latter site also has a directory of other basketball sites of interest.

You don't need to memorize the entire rule book; much of it is for the benefit of coaches, referees, scorekeepers, timekeepers, etc. You do need to know the rules pertaining to dribbling, pivoting, goal tending, defense, traveling, defensive fouls, offensive fouls (what constitutes charging as opposed to blocking), moving picks, fouls off the ball, three-second violations, and the like.

Charging/blocking: An offensive player may not deliberately run into a defensive player who has established position in one spot for a full second or more. This is called "charging." A defensive player may not step into the path of and make contact with an offensive player with the ball; unless he has established that defensive position for at least one second, he may be called for "blocking."

Dribbling: You may use only one hand at a time in dribbling. If you dribble with two hands, or dribble, stop and then resume, these are "double dribbling" violations. If a defensive player knocks the ball out of your hands while you're holding it, however, you may resume dribbling. Anyone may pick up a loose ball and dribble it. Another violation, "palming" the ball, is called when you bounce the ball so high that your hand comes over the top of the ball and you dribble with the palm of your hand as your fingers point downward.

Pivoting: If you are stationary and holding the ball, as soon as you lift one foot, the other foot must remain in place and is called the pivot foot. You may step in any direction with the foot you lifted. For example, if you're holding the ball and step with your right foot, the left foot must remain in place and becomes your pivot foot. It remains the pivot foot until you dribble, pass or shoot. If you move your pivot foot before releasing the ball, it is a "traveling" violation. If you are dribbling, you do not have to keep one foot in place; you may move either foot in any direction you wish.

Traveling: A player who has the ball may not take more than one full step without beginning the motion to dribble, pass or shoot the ball. This motion must be completed before the player completes a second step, otherwise this is a "walking" or "traveling" violation.

Face guard: Means a defensive player directly faces the offensive player he or she is guarding.

Off hand: Refers to the hand not in use when the other hand is occupied in dribbling or shooting. Dribbling or shooting with your right hand, your left hand would be considered your "off" hand.

Pick or Screen (used interchangeably): An offensive player stands in the path of a defender who is guarding a different offensive player for at least one second. The purpose is to cause the defender to lose his man or force him to switch assignments with another defensive player.

Sag: Instead of closely guarding the offensive player he is assigned to guard, a defensive player plays several feet away from that opponent and closer to an offensive player guarded by one of his teammates. A forward or guard will often "sag" to help defend against a center.

Strong side/Weak side: The strong side refers to the side of the court on which there are more offensive players (at least three as opposed to two), and/or to which the ball is moving. The weak side is the side away from the ball and/or the side with fewer offensive players. The strong and weak sides will change as players move from one side of the court to the other.

Model students: Players from Beverly Hills (CA) High School helped me demonstrate the fundamentals illustrated in this book. First row, from left: Chris Gagan, Hannah Novian, Charlene Negari, Henry Choi. Second row: Nate Jones, Hye Jin Jang, Odette Abramovich, the author, Michelle Oglalchehyan, Mariana Correa. Third row: Varsity basketball coach Kevin Brown, Sean Godsick, Nick Montealegre, Kerel Shaffner, Michael Kohan, Henry Fisk, Jason Rofeh. Not in this photo: Anita Kavaei (see her in the "All Purpose Stretch" photos in the chapter on Conditioning); Assistant coach David Goldberg.

A WORD ABOUT GENDER

This book is intended as much for women basketball players as for men. As you'll see throughout the book, young women are in the photos demonstrating fundamentals for us almost as often as young men. In our text, whenever we use the words "he," "his" or "him" as opposed to "he and she," "his and her," etc., we trust you'll understand that we're referring to *all* basketball players regardless of gender, and not just to the male of the species. Wherever possible, we've tried to be gender-neutral but obviously we weren't always successful.

LET ME HEAR FROM YOU!

I'd like to know whether you found THE ART OF BASKETBALL helpful in improving your skills. What kind of progress have you made? How could we make the book better? Do you have questions about anything I've written? Is there anything that's confusing or otherwise difficult to understand? Drop me a line at the address on page 2. We'll try to answer your questions, and we'll put you on our mailing list for news about future publications, events, etc. that might be of interest to you. Or you can send me an e-mail : oscar@thebigo.com.

Okay, enough fooling around. Let's get to work!

PHYSICAL AND MENTAL CONDITIONING

The primary physical attributes you need to play basketball are quickness, strength, endurance and flexibility. The primary mental attributes are concentration, intensity, common sense and confidence.

You need quickness to get open for shots and passes, create moves off the dribble, play defense, and get position for rebounds. You need flexibility to create moves and maneuver around people on offense and defense. You need endurance to go full speed every moment you play and finish even stronger than you started. You need leg strength for a good first step off the dribble, repeated leaping, and position for rebounds and picks. You need upper body strength to pass, dribble, shoot, rebound, and protect the ball. You need the mental attributes to translate the physical skills into winning basketball.

To a degree, quickness and flexibility are determined by your body's muscle and bone structure, connective tissue and neurological system. You can develop quickness and flexibility to your body's maximum capacity. There is virtually no limit to your development of strength and endurance, or the mental attributes required to play the game.

I was blessed with better-than-average height, long arms, good peripheral vision, and good reflexes. However, many players were taller, faster and stronger than me. To compete against them, I knew I had to improve my strength, flexibility and quickness. What you saw of me on a basketball court was the result of years of conditioning, practice and competition. I encourage you to take the same approach. How much you get out of your athletic skill depends on how hard you're willing to work.

MAKE THE COMMITMENT!

The first steps to improving your basketball skills, then, are the same as for any other sport. You have to want to do it, you have to commit to doing it, and you have to take it seriously. If you can associate yourself with other players who are equally dedicated, you'll all improve much faster.

Your own will power and dedication, more than anything else, will determine how much and how fast you improve. Get your body in shape and you'll have a better mental outlook, more confidence in yourself, more command of situations. Develop a winning mental attitude, and self-discipline will take over on those days when that little voice inside you is whining "I'm too tired," "I don't feel like it," or the real killer, "What's the use."

The self-discipline it takes to get out of bed or off your behind every day and work out will serve you throughout life. We tend to be our own biggest obstacles to success. If you can win that one battle each day, you can win the others. You'll feel so good about making yourself work out that soon your mind and body will *demand* that you work out every day.

If you're a youngster, you have a golden opportunity! You can get yourself in shape now to a degree that will serve you for the rest of your life. If you're not so young in body but still young in spirit, you can still begin the re-conditioning process at any time. Your body and mind will respond much faster than you think. Physical and mental conditioning gives you the winning edge, not just in sports, but in everyday life.

10

If you have enough pride in yourself, you'll want to be in good shape whether or not you ever take part in a sport. You'll be less susceptible to illness, and bounce back faster if you do get sick. Being in good shape is not merely a matter of weight. If you're a youngster, your body will go through various stages as it matures. Unless you're seriously obese, your weight is less critical than overall muscle tone and vitality. Your weight and body composition will eventually stabilize.

CONDITIONING YOURSELF TO PLAY BASKETBALL

On the basketball court, a well-conditioned team always has the advantage, even against a team with superior talent. Many a game has been won in the final seconds because one player had the strength left for one last shot, or got a step on a tired opponent and drove for the basket. A basketball game is a series of sprints, but it's also like a marathon. How often have you seen a team spend all its energy to tie a game, then play like slugs in overtime? You have to play hard the entire game, then be able to crank it up even higher at the end. Championship teams do this automatically.

If you're on a team, your coach will have conditioning routines for pre-season and the season itself. You can augment these routines with workouts of your own. In the off-season you can *really* improve if you make a plan and stick to it. From the age of 11, I practiced anywhere from 2–8 hours a day, working on fundamentals as well as physical conditioning. In the summer, I also worked on a farm or on construction projects. Was the investment of time worth it? I wouldn't change a thing.

RUN FOR QUICKNESS, ENDURANCE AND STRENGTH

Because basketball is a running game, conditioning starts with running: distance running for endurance, wind sprints for quickness and endurance. Both will naturally develop a certain amount of leg strength. If you can also run up steep hills, or the steps of a stadium or arena, you can develop even more leg strength and endurance.

If your school has a track team, go out for it. The structured daily workout will do you a world of good, and you'll develop your legs, heart/lung capacity, and coordination. If the coach will help you improve your running technique, that's a bonus. You'd be amazed how many players waste their speed because they never learn to run efficiently.

Soccer is also good for basketball conditioning. The nonstop running, stops, starts and changes of direction are much like basketball. If you can't participate in soccer or track, you should still run on your own. I'm not talking about jogging; I mean actual running, where you extend yourself.

DISTANCE RUNNING

Find an open area—a park, a field, a running track if you're really fortunate—and pace off an eighth, a quarter or a half mile. Walk the route first and check for rocks, holes and sprinkler heads.

Begin your program gradually. You're going to be doing this every day from now on. Stretch before you run. Warm up at half-speed, then go full speed as your lungs open up and you reach your ideal heart rate. Run naturally and easily on the balls of your feet, pump your arms naturally at your sides, breathe in rhythm with your stride.

Once you've found a pace that works, try to run further or a bit faster each day than you did the day before, always at full speed on your last lap. Running fast quarter-miles is a particularly good routine. Run one, walk one. Then get to the point where you can run one, take a quick breather, run another one. If you can run 4–8 fast quarters, then run another two miles at a good steady clip, that's a pretty good endurance running program.

WIND SPRINTS

For basketball, wind sprints are even more valuable than distance running because they develop both quickness and endurance. Football coaches have relied on them for years. These are 40-yard sprints; a basketball court is just a bit over 30 yards at 94 feet, so consider the extra 9 yards a bonus to give you a good finishing kick.

In basketball, a quick first step makes a big difference. Except for fast-break ball where pure speed is valuable in the open court, a quick first step is more important in all other phases of the game.

There were quite a few players in the NBA faster than me, but I always felt confident I could beat anyone with a good fake and a good first step. Wind sprints help you develop the strength, quickness and endurance to explode past your defender, play after play.

Wind sprints also help you develop a change of pace, a critical skill many players never develop. If you always move at the same speed, a defender has a much easier job. You want to keep him back on his heels, reacting and recovering, instead of up on his toes challenging you, coming after the ball. Wind sprints are the foundation for developing a change of speeds.

To run wind sprints, begin from a standing start and sprint as hard as you can for 40 yards. Catch a breath, then sprint again. Shoot for sets of 10 without stopping, and go all out each time. Along with conventional wind sprints, run sideways and backwards as fast as possible without turning your body (keep your feet parallel instead of crossing one over the other), constantly changing directions: left, right, backwards. Linebackers and defensive backs are very familiar with this drill.

RUNNING STEPS AND HILLS

Running steps or uphill—at a football stadium, an arena, any sort of incline—gives you strength in your calves, ankles, quadriceps and hamstrings, four muscle groups you need for basketball. You'll also build endurance and heart/lung capacity. If you don't have steps available, find a steep hill. Run up, walk or jog down. (Running down an incline or steps at full speed is not a good idea.)

ALWAYS RUN WISELY

1. Wear good quality running shoes with plenty of cushion. You may want to add cushioned insoles as well. Try to run on natural surfaces (grass or dirt) rather than hard surfaces (asphalt or concrete). When you run, your foot strikes the ground at 3X the force of your body weight. Your knees and lower back take a lot of pounding if your feet are not properly cushioned.

2. Dress properly: a sweatshirt and sweatpants, unless the weather's simply too hot. If you run in a tank top and shorts, put on sweats when you're finished.

3. Always have water available. While running, sip, drink small amounts, rinse your mouth. After you've cooled down, drink larger amounts to replace the fluids you've lost.

4. Never run full speed without warming up first with stretching exercises and walking or jogging. Running without proper warmup can lead to pulled muscles and other injuries.

5. Don't stop cold. If you run and stop without cooling down properly, you can get cramps. Jog or walk until your breathing returns to normal. A race horse isn't taken back to the barn the minute the race is over; he gallops a bit, then he's covered with a blanket and walked back slowly.

6. Use your common sense when the weather's exceptionally hot or the air quality is unhealthful. I find early morning, or evening just before sundown, the best times of the day for running.

Jumping jacks (left photo), also known as side straddle hops, are a great warmup exercise, equally good for developing legs, wind and endurance. Done properly, they can also develop upper body muscles. The trick is to "reach for the sky" and extend your arms fully every time you bring your hands together over your head. If you "reach" properly, you'll find yourself lighter on your feet and jumping with more spring. Right photo: the arm motion used in jumping jacks can tone the muscles you use in shooting, passing and protecting the ball. Other good exercises for developing important upper body muscle groups include pushups and pullups, along with weight and resistance training.

STRENGTH CONDITIONING

Strength is more important in basketball than many people realize, not only in the inside game, but for protecting the ball in all situations. Quickness can compensate somewhat for a lack of strength, but a complete player needs both leg and upper body strength, especially at forward and center.

Running and certain types of weight training will give you leg strength. Swimming is great for both upper body and leg strength. There are calisthenics that will develop strong arms, wrists and shoulders. The objective is to develop the strength you need without sacrificing flexibility.

At one time, I wasn't too keen on weightlifting, and I'm still not for younger players whose bones and muscles have not yet matured. Never lift weights or work weight machines without proper supervision by a coach or trainer. If you lift free weights, work with a partner. Weight machines can help you develop specific muscle groups without the risk of injury inherent in free weights. I vote for lower weight or resistance and more repetitions as opposed to maximum weight/resistance and fewer reps, because you're working for flexibility and endurance as opposed to power lifting.

Good weight training exercises for basketball? Arm curls. Squats (great for developing ankle, calf, quadricep and hamstring muscles). Knee presses. Military presses. Bench presses (in moderation).

Personally, I prefer calisthenics that use the body's own weight as resistance: pushups, pullups, jumping jacks (side straddle hops), torso twisters, abdominal exercises (situps, leg raises and hip stretches). These basic exercises work just about every muscle group you need. For basketball, there are two additional exercises I feel are essential: hamstring stretches and protecting the ball.

CALISTHENICS

Jumping jacks (side straddle hops) can develop your wind, legs and upper body. The secret is to extend your arms fully and reach for the sky as your hands meet over your head. Feel the stretch in your upper arms and trapezius muscles. Spring into the air off the balls of your feet, spreading your legs as far apart as possible as your hands reach up to touch as far overhead as possible. As you descend, bring your feet together and your arms briskly back down to your sides. You ought to be able to do 50–100 of these rapidly if you're in good shape. Do these first to warm up.

Pushups: Keep your legs and back straight, your rear down and your head up, looking straight ahead. Spread your fingers wide; this will develop your wrists. With your hands directly beneath your shoulders, push straight up and lower yourself slowly, breathing in rhythm. Aim for 100 pushups each morning and night in sets of 10–20 or more. Pushups are great for the muscles you need for shooting, passing, dribbling and rebounding. You cannot do too many pushups.

Pullups develop your back, shoulders, biceps and triceps. The bar should be high enough that your feet do not touch the floor when you hang fully extended. With your hands facing away from your body and spread just a bit wider than your shoulders, take a deep breath and pull yourself straight up, keeping your abdomen sucked in and your legs straight, until your chin is above the bar. Let yourself down slowly. Repeat the exercise as many times as you can in sets of 5–10 or more.

If you can't do any pullups at first, let your body hang limp and relax completely. Take a deep breath and tighten your abdominal muscles. You should always feel a pullup in your abdomen. Pull yourself up slowly, as high as you can, hold yourself there, then let yourself down very slowly (do not drop). This alternative version still does you a lot of good. Once you can pull yourself up all the way over the bar, take a bow! Many people are never able to lift their own body weight. You'll find that once you can do one pullup, the repetitions will come quickly.

Situps help develop your leg, thigh, hip and abdominal muscles. Do them with knees bent to avoid lower back strain. Ask someone to hold your ankles, or use an incline bench with an ankle strap. Clasp your hands behind your head, breathe in, pull your torso into a sitting position with your thigh and abdominal muscles. When you do the exercise properly, you'll feel it first in your thighs. As you sit up, alternate touching right elbow to left knee, left elbow to right knee. Do sets of 10, 15, 20 or more situps, whatever you can manage. A good goal is 100 situps each morning and evening.

Leg raises: Lie flat on your back, legs straight. Inhale deeply and raise one leg straight up. Lower slowly and exhale. Do at least 10 raises for each leg. Keep the other leg bent if that makes it easier.

Hip stretches: Lie flat on your back, legs straight. Inhale deeply, bring one knee or both knees up to your chest. Hold for a count of three. Feel the stretch in your hips, lower back and abdomen as well as your thighs. Exhale and straighten your leg(s) slowly upon return to the floor. Do sets of 10 with each leg and a set of 10 with both legs. Both of these exercises are good for your hips, thighs, abdomen and lower back.

Many people run to build up their heart/lung capacity but neglect their abdomens. Abdominal muscles support the groin and lower back, two areas very vulnerable to injury. You don't need "washboard abs," but you should tone up every day with situps, crunches, leg raises or stretching exercises. You can exercise sitting at home or in a car, just by tightening your abdomen for a count of 10, then relaxing. Good posture gives you a head start in toning these muscles. The older you get, the more you need abdominal exercise.

HAMSTRING STRETCHES

Your thigh muscles (hamstrings and quadriceps) will be in constant use: running, shooting (jump shots and layups), rebounding, holding position, and exploding past a defender with a good first step off the dribble. Running and weights help develop these muscles; this exercise also puts you in the mindset of developing a strong first step. (1) Hold the ball over your head. (2) Pivot on your left foot and step as far to the right as you can, keeping your left leg straight and bending your right knee as much as possible. (3) As you bring your body forward over your right knee, bring the ball from overhead down to your right foot. You'll feel the stretch in both thighs. (4) Swing the ball back up over your head as you stand up. Do sets of at least 10 to each side, alternating pivot feet.

Protecting the ball (above): One player swings the ball in a circle, the other tries to take it away. This drill measures how much you need to improve your upper body strength. Watch the defender's eyes for a preview of his moves.

Hamstring stretches (right): Hamstring and quadricep muscles are critical for basketball. Do this exercise to either side. Bring your body forward over your bent knee. As you stretch, you should bring the ball from overhead to touch your foot.

PROTECTING THE BALL

Any time you have the ball in your hands, there's a good chance a defender will try to steal it. You need upper body strength and quickness to protect the ball. No matter how strong you think you are, test yourself. This exercise duplicates game conditions. (1) Have a teammate face guard you. (2) Crouch with your weight evenly balanced, feet at shoulder width, slightly forward on the balls of your feet. (3) Grip the ball firmly with both hands and move it in a circle, clockwise or counter-clockwise, as your teammate tries to knock the ball out of your hand. (4) Continue until your teammate has knocked the ball out of your hand three times, then switch sides with your teammate.

IMPROVING YOUR VERTICAL LEAP

In rebounding, I consider timing and position both more important than leaping ability. Still, it doesn't hurt to have a good vertical leap. The best way to improve your leap is not with weights or other gizmos, but by jumping as often as possible with as little wasted motion as possible. Extend yourself fully and reach as high as you can. Your lift should come not only from your thigh muscles, but your ankles and calves.

How can you build those muscles? Jumping jacks. Ballet. Run the stairs. Track (high hurdles, low hurdles, high jump, long jump.) Weight training (squats, knee presses). Wind sprints. Get a small portable trampoline and use it indoors. Most important, practice rebounding. Devote plenty of practice time to rebounding instead of spending it all on dribbling and shooting.

CONDITIONING FOR FLEXIBILITY

In basketball, you need flexibility to go with strength and quickness. You rarely have a straight path when you're driving for the hoop, bringing the ball upcourt against the press, playing defense or rebounding. Flexibility comes in handy for blocking shots, stealing passes and dribbles, sliding past picks, executing fakes convincingly, saving a ball that's about to go out of bounds, or getting off a shot or a pass when you're at an angle instead of squared off to your target.

The all-purpose stretch, a variation on a basic yoga exercise, helps you condition practically every muscle in your body. At left, take a deep breath in through your nose and lift your chest. Above and right, extend your arms fully out to the sides, palms up, and bring your hands up over your head.

Stretching exercises are the best way to develop flexibility. Fortunately, stretching is now considered an integral part of conditioning. There are numerous books and videos on stretching, and far more exercises than I can go into here. I recommend you pick five or ten stretches that work the arms, legs, torso, lower back and abdomen. Most stretches are based on yoga exercises thousands of years old. On these pages is the "all-purpose stretch," derived from a basic yoga exercise. Yoga not only helps you develop flexibility and muscle tone, but teaches you to breathe properly.

Calisthenics that work the back and abdominal muscles (situps, leg raises, hip stretches, etc.) are also valuable for developing flexibility, because flexibility in the torso begins with the abdominal muscles. I also recommend (1) touching your toes with your legs spread wide (right hand or both hands to left foot, left or both hands to right foot), while standing or sitting; (2) torso twisters, holding your hands clasped in front of your chest and rotating your torso as far as it will go to either side; and any other exercise that rotates or stretches the torso forward or side to side.

Other sports that help develop flexibility include swimming, diving, fencing and gymnastics. Ballet is wonderful in this regard. Martial arts training can help develop not only flexibility but quickness, self-confidence and self-discipline. Find a teacher who stresses the mental and spiritual aspect of the martial arts as much as the physical, who emphasizes inner strength and self-defense as opposed to offensive tactics designed to injure an opponent.

NUTRITION AND LIFESTYLE

Nutrition and lifestyle affect physical and mental conditioning. Eat properly and drink plenty of water, citrus juices and milk. A good diet includes leafy green and root vegetables, beans, nuts, fish or lean meats, whole grains, and eight glasses of water a day. Avoid chips, fatty foods, deep fried foods and refined sugar. Nothing packaged or canned is as good for you as something natural. You may want to take essential vitamin and mineral supplements. Vitamin C helps you fight off colds and viruses. Calcium builds bones. Potassium (in bananas, apples, other fruits and vegetables) helps muscles and the nervous system. It takes discipline to eat properly instead of cheeseburgers, fries and sodas, but it's worth it. Too many young athletes are dying or having to give up sports because of clogged coronary arteries. Just because you're young doesn't mean you're immune. Everyone's body metabolizes fat in different ways. The best thing to do is avoid it. Restrict fat calories to 10% of your diet even if the American Medical Association guidelines allow 30%.

Keeping your arms fully extended over your head, bend at the waist without bending your knees and touch the floor with your palms or fingertips. Feel the stretch in your upper and lower back, abdomen, thighs and calves. Exhale through your nose as you bend. Stand erect and return to the first position.

Avoid a sedentary lifestyle. Sitting is a killer. Turn off the TV, computer and video games; get out in the fresh air and sunshine whenever possible. When you do read or watch TV, make sure you have proper lighting. Take care of your eyes; they're the only pair you've got. Get plenty of rest. Avoid stress. A problem is a problem only if you think it's a problem. You may have to deal with serious adversity at times, but you have the resources within you to handle it.

Listen to people in authority—parents, teachers, coaches. They can offer you good insights and information. Strive to become as good an athlete as you can, but remember that education is equally important. The same principle applies in the classroom as on the court: Do more than is required of you. Enjoy the learning process as much as you enjoy physical activity. Take pride in being a well-educated athlete instead of the alternative. It makes for a more balanced and successful life.

MENTAL CONDITIONING

In professional sports, the athletes are pretty much equal in terms of ability. What sets the teams that win consistently apart from those that don't? Coaching, to various degrees, but also working as a team and thinking like winners. In basketball, a winner's thinking skills include concentration, intensity, common sense and confidence. Following is a picture of the sort of person I feel is most likely to think like a winner, and consequently to play like one.

- You focus 100% on winning, not on retaliation, showing someone up, or getting even. You welcome the strongest competition. You take the game seriously but enjoy playing the game.

- You stay in control, don't get rattled, don't let an opponent take you out of your game. When there's more pressure, when the game is on the line, that's when you enjoy it the most.

- You deal with reality and adjust to circumstances as they are instead of worrying about what should be. You recognize that the real world includes adversity, mistakes, and the unexpected.

- You motivate yourself because you know that everything you need to win comes from within. You draw encouragement from parents, friends, coaches and teammates, but in the end you take responsibility for yourself.

- You know that another person's opinion does not change what you have inside. You may respect the source of the opinion but you do not have to agree. You never let another person define what you can or cannot achieve.

- You're willing to dream, to set impossible goals and believe you will achieve them, knowing that if you can visualize it, you can do it. Perhaps not exactly when you want, but you can do it. Giving up is not in your vocabulary.

- You focus on doing well what you do best, and improving what you must improve to help your team win. Basketball example: Everyone wants to dunk, including short players; they should be working on ballhandling, defense, outside shooting.

- When the game is over, it's over. No excuses, no blaming others. Did you give your best effort? What do you and your teammates need to do to improve? What time is practice tomorrow?

CONCENTRATION

Concentration is the ability to focus 100% on the task at hand and nothing else. Mental relaxation is the key to concentration. Whatever the situation, whatever the pace of the game, you know how to run it in slow motion in your mind so you can focus better on what you're doing. You block out all distractions and stay within your rhythm; you don't stress, rush or get frantic. You don't let the clock, crowd noise, the background, trash talking, physical intimidation or anything else take you out of your game. Every fundamental of basketball has one or more critical points on which you must focus your attention, consciously or subconsciously, to perform the motions correctly. If you've practiced enough, "muscle memory" should take over the physical aspect of the motions so you can play "in the moment" and concentrate on your goal.

INTENSITY

Intensity means you play the game with the same killer instinct from the opening tipoff to the final buzzer. You only know one way to play, and that's in overdrive. Whatever happened before is over. You're focused only on the moment at hand. You never slack off, never back off, never concede. You don't "take what the defense gives you," because you will not be denied. You adjust, find an opening, attack from a position of strength. Teams who play this way become champions. Teams who play against champions are always looking over their shoulders; they know that no lead is safe because the champs are gonna keep coming at them and will eventually find a way to win.

Whether you're ahead or behind, you never give up. It's a matter of pride. You especially need this quality in playing defense and fighting for rebounds. The moment you admit to yourself that you're beaten, you're beaten. It's that simple. What part of NEVER do you not understand?

COMMON SENSE

Basketball requires intelligence to play well—an intelligence measured not by diplomas, but by the ability to evaluate a situation instantly and make a critical thinking decision. In other words, reasoning, common sense, whatever you call it. Basketball is a very simple game, governed by the laws of physics. For every action, there is an equal and opposite reaction, an if-then scenario. IF you pass into a crowd, THEN a defender will probably steal the ball. IF you take a 30-foot jump shot with a teammate open under the basket, THEN the coach will probably take you out of the game. And so on.

If you concentrate properly, common sense on the court will come naturally. IF you see a problem, THEN the solution is usually in the problem. Of course you'll make mistakes! Learn from them so you don't repeat them. If you don't depend strictly on your athletic skills, but think situations through and make intelligent choices, you'll become a much better player. Soon you won't always have to think things through consciously; making the right choice will become a matter of instinct.

CONFIDENCE

Confidence is not merely a basketball fundamental; it is THE fundamental attribute of successful athletes in any sport and successful persons in all walks of life.

Most players come into the NBA with the same fundamental skills. The confident players, those who show courage and command, who want the ball in pressure situations, are the ones who make the NBA rosters. Those who are hesitant and unsure of themselves are cut loose or ride the bench, even if they have more talent than the players on the court.

You have to believe in yourself before anyone else will. Even if you're not convinced you're as good as the players you face, never let them know it. You gain confidence through competition, but you must also improve with practice on your own so you're prepared for competition when it comes.

Learn from your mistakes! A successful person treats every failure, mistake and rejection as one step closer to his or her goal. If the ball is stolen, you drop a pass, cut the wrong way, miss an open shot or kick the ball out of bounds, what can you do to avoid repeating that mistake? Chances are you'll have the answer immediately. The solution is generally in the problem.

That's why I bring up the subject of confidence here, before I go into any of the fundamentals of the game of basketball. Our purpose from this point on will be not only to develop your skills in executing these fundamentals, but your confidence in these skills as well.

If you follow the physical conditioning guidelines in this chapter, you'll take the first step toward building your confidence. You will have proven to yourself that you can do these things, many of which you may have thought you could not do, and you'll find yourself getting better each day.

A SPECIAL WORD FOR WOMEN ATHLETES

As the husband of a strong, intelligent, independent woman, and the father of three intelligent, strong, independent daughters, I make no claim at all to any special understanding of women. My daughters not only played basketball well, but were outstanding all-around athletes; none of them chose to pursue basketball, which was their choice to make.

In 1964, we brought out an earlier version of this book called PLAY BETTER BASKETBALL. At that time, there was no women's basketball on the scale you have today. Few coed colleges had women's teams, and there were no women's pro leagues, at least in the United States. The emergence of women basketball players at both the college and pro level is a development I heartily applaud. If you're a young woman of any age who enjoys playing basketball, follow your dream! This book is for you every bit as much as it is for male athletes.

In addressing this book to women as well as men, and focusing not only on the physical game but the mental, I got an unexpected assist from my former Boston Celtics adversary K.C. Jones, one of the smartest men ever to step on a basketball court. As this book was written, K.C. was coaching the New England Blizzard in the American Basketball League, and was quoted in a *Los Angeles Times* story by Earl Gustkey as follows:

"Other than the obvious stuff like size and strength, I'd say the work ethic and the enthusiasm in the women's game are much better. The big difference is the confidence. Men have it, the women don't. I have to keep boosting my players' confidence. Carla Berube—she has no idea how talented she is. I have to draw it out of her. Same with Kara Wolters. She's slow, but so was Larry Bird. She has good feet and hands. Her upside is awesome. Yet she has very little confidence."

It's my impression that women go through various steps on the road to confidence, which are:

"I can't do this."

"Should I do this?"

"I hope I can do this."

"Hey, maybe I *can* do this."

"Hey, I'm pretty good at this!"

Women have been conditioned for generations to take a secondary role, not to be assertive. Even though women have proven themselves to be superb athletes in many individual sports, it may not be easy to change your behavior and mental outlook in team sports which *demand* assertiveness and confidence. The first thing you do is erase all self-doubt. Then, as you begin to condition yourself to play basketball, pay special attention to the mental aspects of the game at the same time as you're improving yourself on the athletic side. In particular, to repeat what I said in "Think Like a Winner," never let anyone else define who you are and what you can or cannot do.

YOUR DAILY CONDITIONING CHECKLIST

For both men and women of all ages, I hope you'll apply the same determination and work ethic to the remaining lessons in this book that you apply to physical and mental conditioning. If you do that, you'll be able to develop your skills and your confidence at the same time!

Try to work out an hour or more a day in addition to the practice time you devote to basketball fundamentals. Split the workout into morning and evening segments if that works better for your schedule. Your conditioning workout should include as many of the following as possible:

___ Running for distance

___ Wind sprints: straight ahead, laterally and backward

___ Running up stairs or hills

___ Weight training (every other day or three times a week instead of daily)

___ Basic calisthenics: Jumping jacks, pushups, pullups, situps, abdominal exercises

___ Stretching exercises

___ Hamstring stretches

___ Protecting the ball

DEFENSE

Defense is more than part of the art of basketball; it is the *heart* of basketball. It takes heart to play winning defense, because you never give up. The physical and mental conditioning required to play defense will serve you well in all other aspects of the game.

The most successful franchise in basketball was built around a player who was a poor shooter, but the greatest rebounder and defensive player the game has ever known. The team was the Boston Celtics and the player was Bill Russell. The Celtics won 11 NBA championships during Russell's 13 years as a player, a record unequalled in any other sport. Other great centers were active at the time—Wilt Chamberlain, Walt Bellamy and Nate Thurmond, for example—but only one Russell.

Russell was 6'9"—average height for a center even then—and skinny as a rail, but he was a champion high-jumper. More important, he always seemed to be where the ball was. If you drove to the basket, he was there to block your shot or force you to alter the shot. Blocked shots were not kept as a statistic in those days, but I have never seen anyone block or disrupt as many shots as he did.

Boston's entire game revolved around Russell. Its guards and forwards played aggressive defense and gambled for steals, knowing that if an opponent got past them, Russell was in the lane to take away the drive. The Boston fast break usually began with an outlet pass from Russell after a rebound, sometimes with one of his court-length inbounds passes after the other team had scored.

With Russell leading the way, the Celtics also helped bring about an evolution in the philosophy of playing defense. Up to that point, the idea had been to hold the other team to one shot, stop them from scoring and get the rebound. The Celtics' philosophy was to attack the other team, exploit its weaknesses and try to get the ball back before the other team even had a chance to shoot. Playing defense this way is a lot more work, and a lot of teams are not willing to work that hard.

DEFENSE SETS THE TONE OF THE GAME

When two teams are equal in shooting ability and shot selection, the better defensive team always has the advantage. If you play good, aggressive defense, you can set the tone of the game. You can disrupt the other team's offense, force turnovers, take them out of their game. You can make them lose composure, hurry their shots and passes. Defense is a mind game as well as a physical game. And it's fun to play! Everyone is involved. On offense, only one person at a time has the ball.

If you and your teammates take a team approach to playing defense, always communicating, helping each other, constantly making adjustments, you'll play together better on offense as well. Playing this style of defense makes you a stronger team, and lets the other team know you intend to battle them at both ends of the court.

In its simplest terms, defense is a matter of preparation and perspiration. You have to know your opponent, and dog him/her every second you're on the court. You don't need superhuman talent to do this, just the personal pride and will power to stick to the task. This means you're always alert, moving, adjusting, helping and communicating with your teammates, giving 100% at all times. If you want to be a complete basketball player, defense must be part of your regular practice routine, along with studying your opponents whenever possible so you're better prepared to play them.

LEARN FROM THE BEST!

If you want to improve your defense, volunteer to guard the best player on the other team. You may get beaten from time to time, but you'll also learn what sets the good players apart from average players. You'll learn how to recognize your opponent's strengths and weaknesses, tendencies and habits. You'll learn how to make adjustments against taller and quicker opponents, and make them work harder for shots, passes and rebounds. Most important, you're conditioning yourself to think like a winner by seeking and responding to a challenge.

MY CASE AGAINST THE ZONE DEFENSE

I should make it clear that defense to me means man-to-man. Too many coaches take the challenge, the aggressiveness and the fun out of defense by playing a zone. (In a zone defense, players are responsible for covering certain zones, or areas of the court, converging on the player who has the ball within that area.) The usual excuse coaches give is that they don't have time to teach man-to-man defense, or they have a height disadvantage, a quickness disadvantage, or whatever.

In a zone defense, you play the ball and move according to the movement of the ball. A man-to-man defense not only requires closer communication with your teammates, it's also a personal battle between you and your opponent. It's your responsibility to keep the ball away from your opponent and keep him from scoring if he does get the ball. If you are required to play a zone, play it with the same killer instinct as if you were playing man-to-man.

The zone defense is not permitted in the NBA. Even if it were, I doubt many coaches would use it, because a good passing team that moves the ball crisply can always beat a zone defense. Nor can a zone defense generally neutralize a good outside shooting team.

FIVE KEYS TO GREAT DEFENSE

Aggressiveness, quickness, preparation, communication and tenacity are the keys to playing good defense. Height helps close to the basket, but you can compensate for lack of height with quickness and by communicating with your teammates so you help each other.

1. AGGRESSIVENESS

Aggressiveness does not mean you play dirty or play an extremely physical game. It means you play with intensity and attack the other team instead of reacting to what they do. You anticipate and challenge every move. You deny your opponent the ball. You press to make him stop his dribble. You deny him the shot he wants. You block him off the boards. You make him work harder than he wants to work and you take him out of his game! That's how you play aggressive defense.

2. QUICKNESS: USE TWO HANDS AND TWO FEET

Quickness is more important in playing defense than pure speed. Speed is valuable in the open court, but more of the game is played in the forecourt than the open court. Wind sprints and agility drills will help you develop quickness. If you're on a team, your coach will probably run agility drills. Work on those drills on your own outside of practice as well! When you run wind sprints, also run laterally (sideways) and backwards as fast as possible while still keeping your balance. Constantly change speeds and directions. That's what you'll be doing on the court.

However hard you work to develop your quickness, there will still be times when you have to guard a quicker opponent. How can you compensate and keep the advantage?

The basic defensive stance: (left) Slight crouch, arms extended, weight balanced and slightly forward on the balls of your feet, knees bent. You're ready to move both feet in any direction. You can't play defense standing upright, flatfooted, legs straight (at right); you have to be in a crouch, knees bent. Otherwise it's too easy for an opponent to pull you off balance or catch you back on your heels.

To play winning defense, you must **(1)** use two hands and two feet; **(2)** move your feet first, not your body; and **(3)** *always move both feet!* No matter what moves your opponent makes in whatever direction, you have to move both feet to stay ahead of him!

The usual tendency is to react to an opponent's first move by taking one long step in the same direction your opponent moves. The minute you do that, you're off balance. You have to crouch, keep your knees bent, keep your feet spread about the width of your shoulders, stay up on the balls of your feet, and spring with both feet in whatever direction you move. Moving both feet at the same time makes all the difference in the world.

Many defenders forget they have a left hand. If you're guarding a righthander, your left hand is closer to the ball when he dribbles, passes or shoots, and can "mirror" what he does with his right hand. You'll find it easier to block shots, bat away passes or steal the dribble with your left hand. That's one of the reasons Bill Russell was so effective as a shot-blocker, because he was using his dominant (left) hand playing against righthanded shooters.

3. PREPARATION: KNOW YOUR OPPONENT

You play defense with your head as well as your hands and feet. If you learn your opponent's habits, tendencies, preferences, strengths and weaknesses, you can make adjustments on defense before your opponent realizes you're on to what he's doing. If you're on a team, you'll usually get scouting reports, but there's no substitute for watching or playing against an opponent in person.

What are your opponent's preferred shooting spots? What fakes does he use most often? Does he move without the ball, or stand and wait for someone to pass the ball to him? Can he dribble with either hand and in either direction? Does he look at the ball when he dribbles? Can he dribble when he's closely guarded, or does he give up the ball? Can he get open for shots one-on-one, or does he have to come off a screen? Does he pass to open teammates, or look only for his own shots? Does he force shots or passes? Does he always pass in a certain direction? Will he drive for the basket, or does he shy away from physical contact and shoot only from outside?

Half the battle is knowing, or being able to anticipate, what your opponent is going to do. Smart players keep a "book" on other players. You'll notice in the NBA that as players get older, the good ones make up for any loss of quickness with added smarts. A hotshot rookie may make a veteran look bad once, but he probably won't do it again. It takes only one swing around the league for the veterans to size up the new players. From then on it's competition on more equal terms.

4. COMMUNICATION: TALK TO YOUR TEAMMATES

Silence on defense is deadly. It leads to easy baskets for your opponent and costly fouls for your side. Most breakdowns happen because teammates don't talk to each other. You have to call picks, and call for help when your man gets past you, you're screened out, or you're overmatched (for example, a taller opponent takes you into the pivot). Offenses are *designed* to pick off defenders and create mismatches. You can't be too proud to call for help; you and your teammates have to let each other know what's happening at all times. If you don't communicate, you're giving the other team a big advantage.

5. TENACITY: NEVER GIVE UP

Tenacity means simply that you never give up—even when your tongue is hanging out and you think you can't take another step! Refusal to surrender is part of a winning attitude. This is mental conditioning. You never show fear, you never show desperation, you never concede anything. You stick to your opponent like glue and make him or her give up, give less than a total effort, or become angry. If he does any of these things, you've taken him out of his game!

THE BASIC DEFENSIVE STANCE

Take up this stance facing your opponent, about an arm's length away (unless you're guarding a center, in which case you'll often play behind him). If you play closer than an arm's length, you're too easy to screen out and too easy to drive around. Much further away, you're conceding the shot and allowing your opponent to receive passes unchallenged. You have to know how much of a shooting threat your opponent is, and from which areas of the court.

- Arms: Relaxed but ready to extend fully in any direction.
- Feet: Spread to about the width of your shoulders. This makes it easier to move both feet.
- Knees: Bent slightly so you're in a crouch.
- Weight: Evenly balanced, slightly forward on the balls of your feet.

From this stance, you should be able to react quickly in any direction—laterally (side to side), forward, backward—and still keep your weight evenly balanced. You can't react quickly if you're off balance. You can't be caught back on your heels, or you're already beaten.

You cannot play defense flatfooted or with your legs straight. A slight crouch with your weight slightly forward on the balls of your feet gives you a lower center of gravity and more spring in your step. Most of the time you'll move laterally. Whatever direction you move, your weight must remain evenly balanced, and you must *move both feet at the same time* instead of first lunging with your body or taking a step with only one foot. Don't think in terms of stepping with two feet at the same time; think in terms of springing or hopping on both feet to get into the position you want.

Moving both feet at the same time is one of the basics of playing defense. That's how you stay a step ahead of any move your opponent makes. It's easier to do this if you stay in a crouch, knees bent, up on your toes. If the ball-handler in the left photo cuts back to her right, the defender is ready to spring in that direction with both feet and keep her feet moving. Here's what happens if you move only one foot instead of two (photo at right): you've committed to moving right, and you're off balance. If your opponent has faked you and cuts back to his right, he's a step or two ahead before you can shift your weight and recover.

If you (1) turn your body without first moving your feet, (2) move only one foot instead of two, (3) cross your legs, (4) turn your back to your opponent, or (5) jump before your opponent moves, you invite your opponent to put all kind of moves on you. You want to *face* him and stay a step in front, whatever direction he moves. Your position in relation to your opponent is more critical than your height or the length of your arms.

DEALING WITH FAKES

Suppose your opponent has a lot of moves and fakes. How do you keep from being faked out? You cannot be overanxious; keep your head up and be alert. If you watch only your opponent's feet, he can fake you. If you watch his head and shoulders, he can fake you. If you watch the ball, he can fake you. You have to use your peripheral vision to play defense: while keeping the ball in view, concentrate on a spot your opponent cannot move without moving his body in that direction.

Watch your opponent's belt buckle. He can fake with his head, shoulders, feet, arms, or the ball, but he can't move his midsection without moving the rest of his body in that direction. At the same time, watch the ball, your teammates and your opponents out of the corners of your eyes.

If you *are* faked and your opponent gets past you, you must call for help, and quickly pick up the man your teammate was guarding before he picked up your man.

USING YOUR HANDS

Unless he has the ball, always keep a hand between your opponent and the ball. If your opponent has the ball, position your hands according to what he's doing. If he dribbles, keep your arms wide and your hands low. If he's holding the ball, keep both arms fully extended, or one hand in his face, the other hand to the side where he's holding the ball so you can challenge his pass or his shot.

Two hands, two feet: Move both feet to keep your balance and cut off your opponent (left photo). The defender correctly uses his left hand to mirror the dribbler's right hand. The dribbler protects the ball properly but helps the defense by not keeping his head up.

Know your opponent: Is she more likely to pass, shoot or dribble in this situation (right photo)? The defender plays back to cut off the pass and help whoever's guarding the pivot. I'd prefer she were just a bit closer and in more of a crouch with her weight forward.

When should you try to steal your opponent's dribble? Hopefully, you've studied your opponent enough to anticipate his reactions. If you go for the ball and he reacts quickly enough, you could make contact with his arm instead of the ball and draw a foul. Use your left hand for a cleaner shot at the ball. There are times when, depending on who you're guarding, you may *want* your opponent to keep dribbling while your teammates keep other players from getting the ball.

In a shooting situation, you should have a hand in your opponent's face, or have both arms up to challenge a pass or a shot. If your opponent goes up for a shot, get your hands up as high as you can. Unless you have an absolutely clear shot at the ball, do not go for the ball if he has it above his head, otherwise you risk drawing a foul. Do keep your hands as high as possible so he has to shoot over them. Also do whatever else you can legally to distract him—yell, wave your arms, whatever.

Common mistakes: Never turn your back on your opponent (photo at left). With one step to his right, the ball-handler is on his way to the basket before the defender can recover. He's also wide open to shoot or pass in practically any direction. In the photo at right, the defender has her opponent tied up? Wrong—she hasn't moved forward on the balls of both feet; her weight is back on her heels and she's off balance. If the ball-handler drops or pulls down the ball, she can re-start her dribble or draw the defender into a foul.

BLOCKING SHOTS

Many people think defense means merely blocking shots. Of course, there's much more to it than that: Denying your opponent the ball, denying his favorite shooting spots, forcing bad shots.

If you *establish* that you can block shots, you can take away the opposition's inside game and force them into lower-percentage outside shots. The threat of a blocked shot, the intimidation factor, is just as important as the block itself.

I think one reason you see so many dunks today, or so many players trying to dunk, is that there are no more Bill Russells, Wilt Chamberlains or Nate Thurmonds in the pivot playing defense. I'm surprised more players don't look for the driving shot first instead of the three-pointer. Many coaches, however, do not want their guards to penetrate, but to stay back and deny the fast break.

Blocking a jump shot is more difficult than blocking a layup, because the shooter knows when he's going to jump. Most blocked jumpers are caused by carelessness or arrogance on the part of the shooter. He didn't make sure he was open before he shot; he hesitated too long and tipped off the defender; or he tried to force a shot in a situation where he should have passed.

Blocking shots can be risky even when you have the timing and/or height advantage, because you can make a clean block and still get called for a foul by an incompetent official. Two suggestions: (1) Mirror your opponent. If he's shooting with his right hand, go for the block with your left hand, so you don't have to reach across his body. In particular, when your opponent is driving for the hoop and you're matching him stride for stride, you have a better chance of a clean block if you jump off your "mirror" pivot foot and use your "mirror" hand. (2) Instead of trying to block the ball in your opponent's hand, jump straight up and block the shot in the air. If you jump toward the shooter, your momentum will probably carry you into a collision with him.

DENYING YOUR OPPONENT THE BALL

Denying your opponent the ball is your first objective in playing defense. No one can score without the ball. When you're playing an opponent without the ball, you have to keep between your opponent and the ball, and between your opponent and the basket.

If your opponent is taller, you'll be at somewhat of a disadvantage, because the other team can lob passes over your head. But you can still contain your opponent—keep him away from his favorite shooting spots, stop his dribble so he has to give up the ball to a teammate.

Of course, some players handle the ball as part of their jobs—guards, for example, who bring the ball upcourt. If you're assigned to a guard who's a good outside shooter, or who likes to penetrate to the basket, you want to challenge his dribble and make him give up the ball, and then stick with him so he can't get it back. If the guard is not a scoring threat from outside, your strategy may be to play back and try to intercept or disrupt his passes.

Where should you pick up your opponent? That depends on his capabilities and on the type of defense your coach prefers. If you're playing a full or halfcourt press, you pick up your man at the other end of the court or the center line. Otherwise you generally pick him up somewhere between the center line and the top of the key. If the other team likes to shoot three-pointers, then you may want to pick up the three-point shooters higher than usual. The higher you pick up an opponent, the longer the pass he has to throw and the better your chances of intercepting the pass. The disadvantage in picking someone up too high is that if he gets past you, that creates a switch or an overload for your teammates closer to the basket.

Denying your opponent the ball: You have to stay between your opponent and the ball, between your opponent and the basket, and make sure you can see both your opponent and the ball. Keep your head up and use your peripheral vision to see the entire flow of play. When you watch only the ball (right photo), your opponent can easily slip past you. Because she stepped toward the ball with only one foot, the defender now has to shift her weight quickly to her left and move both feet to catch up with her opponent.

DENYING YOUR OPPONENT'S FAVORITE SPOTS

An important defensive tactic is to beat your opponent to the spots on the court where he prefers to shoot. You'll often use this tactic against an opponent who's quicker than you, a good outside shooter and also a threat to drive to the basket. The idea is to take away at least one of his options (the outside shot) with the understanding that you'll get some help from your teammates if he decides to go for the hoop.

When you're watching a game, you'll notice that almost every player has one or two favorite spots on the court where he shoots. In fact, there are probably plays designed to get him the ball at those spots. Some players will shoot whenever they're in the corner. Others prefer the top of the key, the foul line, or just to the right or left of the foul line. Players insist they don't have any favorite spots, or they may not be conscious of always shooting from certain spots. But almost everyone will show some kind of pattern in his shooting preferences. As a defender, it's your obligation to learn those patterns and take your opponent out of his game.

OVERPLAYING YOUR OPPONENT

Here's another defensive tactic you need to learn, especially if you're a guard: how to overplay your opponent. (If you're playing defense in the pivot, it's almost automatic that you'll overplay.)

When he has the ball, a righthanded player tends to move to his right, a lefthander to his left. If you guard your opponent straight on, you give him the advantage of the first step in going the way he wants to go.

So what you have to do is "overplay" your opponent, that is, play him slightly to his favorite side. If he's righthanded, you line up with your head even with his right shoulder. If he's lefthanded, you line up even further than that to his left side. You want to force him opposite the direction he prefers to go. Unless he can dribble equally well with both hands, he probably will not try to beat you in the direction you've overplayed, and give up the ball. If he dribbles away from you, you've still cut down his chances of getting off a shot, because he probably won't be as comfortable moving opposite the direction he prefers.

Overplaying: When you know your opponent's capabilities and tendencies, you can force him out of his game by overplaying him. If your opponent always wants to go to his right, and can't dribble with his left hand, you overplay to the right and force him to his left. If he's lefthanded, he's probably even weaker at going to his right, so you overplay him to the left. The risk in overplaying is that you can get beaten by a crossover dribble, but if you've studied your opponent, you should already know whether he has that capability.

If you overplay an opponent and he dribbles straight at you, you have a clear shot at stealing the ball. If he dribbles away from you using the hand closer to you (for example, he dribbles to his left using his right hand), you have an equally good opportunity for a steal. This is where the value of overplaying your opponent is greatest.

In the chapter on dribbling, I emphasize the importance of dribbling equally well with either hand. A righthanded player who can dribble to his left has a distinct advantage over a defender who overplays him to the right. Very early in my development as a player, I made a decision to master going to my left. I soon found myself shooting my jump shot much more often moving to my left than moving to my right, and because I was moving away from the defender, the shot became that much more difficult to block. In fact, once I mastered going to my left, I could probably count on one hand the number of times I had a jump shot blocked.

DEFENDING AGAINST GUARDS

Playing defense as a guard is much more demanding than at forward or center, because you're on the move all the time and you're constantly making decisions while you're on the move. You have to be quick, smart and aggressive to play defense successfully at the guard position.

As a guard, you'll be dealing with a lot of screens and picks, which lead to switched assignments and mismatches. You'll often find yourself guarding a taller player who wants to take you inside.

Many teams begin their halfcourt offense with the guards crossing, one guard screening for the other, or a forward coming up to screen for a guard. In situations such as this, should you stay with your man or switch assignments with a teammate? If it's a good shooting situation for the other team, you're probably better off switching; up higher on the court, try to stay with your man. Your coach may tell you what he prefers you to do. If he leaves the choice up to you, obviously you and your teammates have to let each other know what to do.

Steals (above): It's always tempting to go for a steal, especially when the ball-handler is dribbling too high and isn't protecting the ball with her body. However, the defender shouldn't have turned her body (now the ball-handler can execute a crossover dribble past her on the left), and could have used her left hand to go for the steal, which would have given her a cleaner shot at the ball.

Boxing out (left): Part of your defensive assignment, especially in the forecourt, is to block your opponent off the boards. Use your quickness to get between your opponent and the basket; use hip and leg strength to maintain position. Keep your hands in the air and be ready to move in any direction for the rebound.

DEFENDING AGAINST FORWARDS

If you're guarding a forward or a center, you'll be expected not only to keep your opponent from scoring, but to get good floor position so you can rebound. You have to play both the ball and your opponent. This requires quickness and concentration.

Many forwards do not put enough effort into their defense. They play back from their opponent, and don't really put up a challenge until he has the ball. By then it may be too late. He's already gotten off the shot, or he fakes you into committing a stupid foul. If you play him closer, you'll be in a better position to keep him from getting the ball, or from setting up in a favorite shooting spot. This takes more work, but it's worth it.

A forward may not dribble as much as a guard, but he will move more without the ball to get into position for a shot. Plays are often set up to spring a forward loose for a shot as he moves toward the basket. Your job is to stay between him and the basket, and between him and the ball. Keep your hands up so you can challenge passes in his direction instead of conceding them.

Forwards are just as likely to drive off the dribble as guards. A forward who can shoot from outside and drive to the hoop is much more difficult to guard than one who plays a stationary game. (Elgin Baylor was a master of this inside/outside game, and many other agile big men also come to mind.) Once you know whether or not your opponent can dribble (and many forwards can't), you'll know how tight or loose to play him.

If your opponent is equally good at shooting from outside or going to the basket, you should first try to deny him the ball at his favorite shooting spots. If he does get the ball, then you will have to use your best judgement whether to challenge the outside shot or lay back a bit and try to take away the drive to the basket.

Defense in the pivot: You almost always overplay to one side or the other and try to force the center opposite the direction he'd prefer to go. Keep a hand up to challenge the pass, and be ready to move quickly with both feet to cut off his path to the basket as the pivotman moves in the direction of the pass. Whoever's guarding the forward on this side of the court could sag to help out, unless the forward has the ball. Once the pass comes into the pivot (right photo), you have to react quickly. Here, the defender moved as soon as the pivotman got the ball, and cut off the baseline, cut off the inside move, and is in a good position to challenge a jump shot.

DEFENSIVE PLAY IN THE PIVOT

Guarding a center is a special challenge. Instead of face guarding your opponent, you'll often play behind him. A center usually sets up with his back to the basket, with all the action in front of him, and he can move in any direction to receive a pass, pass to a teammate or screen for a teammate. The main factors that determine your defensive strategy are your opponent's quickness, mobility, height and repertoire of shots. Can he shoot free throws? Play in the pivot is going to be physical anyway, and if you foul someone, it may as well be a poor free throw shooter.

In the pivot, you play the man first and the ball second, and you generally overplay the man. A right-handed center will generally pivot first to his left in shooting a hook shot or a turnaround jumper, or driving to the basket. So you overplay him on his left and force him back to his right. But you can't overplay too much, otherwise he can turn to the basket for a pass from a teammate.

It's rarely a good idea to play in front of a center. If he's taller, his teammates can lob the ball over your head. And what's to prevent him from circling in front of you, or breaking toward the basket?

Your teammates, however, can help you keep the ball away from the center; for example, the guard or forward who's away from the ball can sag toward the lane. Your primary mission is to stay between the center and the basket at all times, and keep him as far from the basket as possible. You especially want to keep him away from the offensive board. You have to be aware of where the ball is at all times and react accordingly when a player on the other team takes a shot.

Another responsibility of pivot defense is to pick up an opponent who has gotten past one of your teammates and is driving for the basket, which puts you in the middle of a 2-on-1. You have to develop an instinct for when to go for the blocked shot, when to challenge the pass, when to play for the rebound.

A smaller player can successfully guard a taller player, even in the pivot. In your pickup games, guard taller players and see what works for you in terms of cutting down their scoring and rebounding opportunities. As I've mentioned before, you should play against players of all sizes and skill levels, because nothing sharpens your defensive skills like competition.

Centers have actually made the defense's job easier today. Few can shoot the hook shot, let alone shoot it with either hand. Some shoot a turnaround jumper, which can be difficult to stop unless you use your "mirror" hand. Many centers today can't even play facing away from the basket. Most of them are looking primarily for the dunk, and their game consists of whatever moves they have to the basket, with or without the ball.

PLAYING DEFENSE AS A TEAM

In addition to guarding your own man, your responsibilities on defense include calling out and reacting to picks and screens, switching defensive assignments as necessary, and picking up the open man. Depending on your position, they could also include blocking out underneath the boards, sagging off your man to help a teammate, double-teaming and pressing.

The two main rules of playing defense as a team are (1) be alert at all times, and (2) communicate. Talking to each other on defense is critical. One of the most unfortunate aspects of the game today is "talking trash." Too many players are so concerned with ragging on whoever they're guarding that they don't pay enough attention to communicating with their teammates.

Sometimes you may be screened out and your man gets open. Or your man drives past you. In a situation such as this, you have to call, "My man! Help out!" And you can't stand still while you do this; you must pick up whoever else is open as quickly as possible. Never be ashamed to call for help on defense. You're part of a team; you help each other.

WHEN TO SAG

If you're a guard or forward, and your opponent is not much of a scoring threat from outside, you might "sag"—that is, play back from him and closer to a forward or center—especially if the forward or center is taller, stronger or quicker than your teammate who's guarding him.

Sometimes your coach has you sag because he wants a defender in front of as well as behind the other team's center at all times. Sometimes you may choose to sag on your own; if your opponent is a poor passer or telegraphs his passes, for example, you can back off a step or two and steal the ball.

The main reason you sag is to make it more difficult for the other team to pass the ball to a certain player. You gamble that the player you've left unguarded will not be able to hit the outside shot. When there were a lot of good outside shooters in the NBA, you could get burned by sagging off the wrong player. Today there aren't as many good outside shooters. Sure, there are three-point specialists, but there are few teams whose players can all hit consistently from outside.

WHEN TO DOUBLE-TEAM

There may be times when, instead of sagging, your coach wants you to go after the player who has the ball even if you aren't assigned to guard that player. This is called double-teaming, and can be especially effective against poor shooters or ball handlers. If your team plays a pressing defense, double-teaming is often part of the strategy. If you're called upon to double-team, you have to be quick enough to get back and pick up your own man when he gets the ball, or have a defensive rotation worked out ahead of time so that another one of your teammates picks up your man.

Common mistakes: You can't let your opponent get even one step inside of you. Above, as soon as the pass was in the air, the defender should have moved left because a righthander with his back to the basket will generally pivot first to his left. Strength is no substitute for quickness and moving both feet. At right, the defender has stepped out too far and given her opponent a clear path to the basket; all she has to do is turn and catch the pass.

One situation that almost always calls for a double-team is when an opponent, usually a guard, has the habit of turning his back to his defender while dribbling. This offers a second defender, usually the offside forward, an opportunity to move in undetected and steal the ball. Sometimes an offensive player will deliberately turn his back to draw a double-team so one of his teammates can get open. Before you go for the steal on a double-team, you have to know where your man is.

WHEN TO PRESS

If the other team can't handle the ball well, why allow them to bring it up the court unchallenged? A pressing defense can slow down a good ball-handling team and totally disrupt a team that can't handle the ball well. Pressing means you start guarding your opponents at the other end of the court (full court press) or at the center line (half court press). You can press man-to-man, double-teaming, or zone; press only their ball-handlers or all their players. It's important to have your defensive rotation worked out in advance so you know who is responsible for which opponents.

DEFENDING AGAINST PICKS AND SCREENS

A "pick" means that an opponent other than the one you're guarding stands in your path to block you momentarily while your opponent gets open. The player setting the pick or screen (the terms are used interchangeably) must establish position a full second ahead of you and stand still. If you make hard contact with him, you can be charged with a foul. (If he has to move to stay in your path, he can be charged with a "moving pick," also a violation but rarely called by the officials.)

Picks or screens are set to (1) create mismatches as defenders switch assignments; (2) free up a ball-handler closely guarded by a defender; (3) set up a shot for a player coming off the screen; (4) allow a player moving without the ball to get open for a shot. Usually a center or forward will come out to the foul line or alongside the lane and set a pick for the guard who's handling the ball.

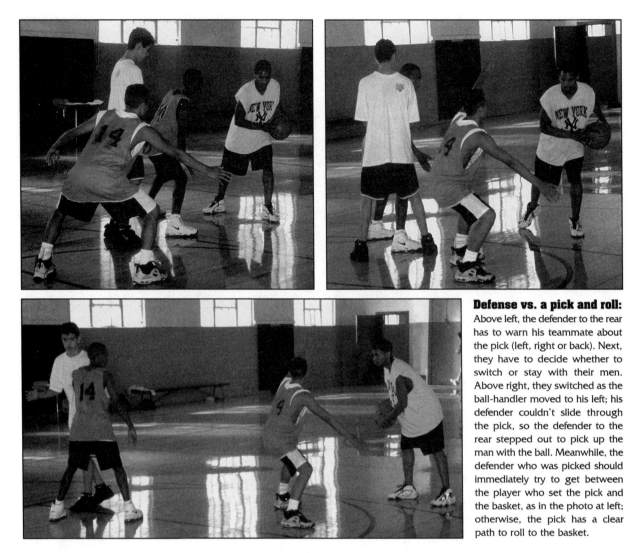

Defense vs. a pick and roll: Above left, the defender to the rear has to warn his teammate about the pick (left, right or back). Next, they have to decide whether to switch or stay with their men. Above right, they switched as the ball-handler moved to his left; his defender couldn't slide through the pick, so the defender to the rear stepped out to pick up the man with the ball. Meanwhile, the defender who was picked should immediately try to get between the player who set the pick and the basket, as in the photo at left; otherwise, the pick has a clear path to roll to the basket.

When a pick is set in your path, should you switch assignments, or fight through the pick and stay with your man (also called "sliding")? Ideally, you want to slide through in front of the pick. Or, your teammate steps back and you slide behind the pick. This move, however, gives the player with the ball an opportunity to stop immediately behind the pick and take an unguarded shot.

If the opponent you're guarding sets a pick, alert your teammate who's being picked off. Call out "pick left," "pick right" or "pick back" to let him know where the pick is being set. If a pick is set in your path, the teammate guarding the player who sets the pick must warn you in the same manner.

Then you and your teammate have to let each other know whether to switch assignments, or if there's room for the player being picked to "slide" in front of or behind the pick and stay with his man. The player who calls the pick should call "slide" or "go through." "Switch" can be either player's call because the player who's picked generally has a better idea whether he can get through. In a shooting situation, it's usually better to switch; higher up, try to stay with your man.

STOPPING THE PICK AND ROLL

Often, a player sets a pick, turns to the basket as soon as the defenders switch, and receives a pass from the player with the ball. This is called a "pick and roll." Many defenders have trouble against it, even at the highest levels of the game. The player who sets the pick is often taller than the man who picks him up, and already has a step toward the basket. The best way to beat a "pick and roll" is to step back as you switch, so you can deny the man who set the pick a clear path to the basket.

Left photo, the ball-handler is moving right (the defender's left). If his defender can't fight through the pick, he has to turn quickly (above) to cut off the pick's path to the basket after the switch.

Few things are as frustrating as to be screened out of a play, or to be caught in a "pick and roll," because a teammate didn't warn you that a pick was in your path. Coaches have been known to bench players who don't call picks for their teammates.

All this talk of picks and screens may be thoroughly confusing if you've played in nothing but pickup games, where players generally don't set picks. In organized competition, however, screens and picks are a basic part of offensive play, and quick reaction to those picks is an essential part of playing defense. If you and your teammates talk, you can eliminate 80% of the confusion and breakdowns that happen on defense when teammates don't talk.

Good defense requires cooperation and communication. Particularly if you play the pivot, you have the play in front of you and you can let your teammates know what's happening. Whatever position you play, call the picks and demand that your teammates do likewise.

WHAT TO DO IN A MISMATCH

If you're picked off and have to switch assignments, you'll often wind up guarding a taller player who wants to take you to the basket. Call for help! It's unlikely you'll stop him by yourself, unless you're quick enough to knock the ball away cleanly, so don't be ashamed to ask for help.

Sometimes you may be called upon to foul the taller player instead of giving up an easy basket—especially if that player is a poor free throw shooter and/or you're not in foul trouble. It may be better to take a chance on that player making two free throws than to concede a sure basket to him.

DEFENDING AGAINST THE FAST BREAK

The transition from offense to defense, particularly when the other team likes to run, presents a special challenge. Many coaches today keep their guards back on offense instead of allowing them to penetrate or to follow their own missed shots, so the guards can get back quickly on defense.

When the opposition fast breaks, one or more players might be halfway down the court before you can react. In this situation, you don't worry as much about picking up your usual opponent as you do about stopping the lead men on the fast break. You may need to alert a teammate to pick up your man while you take his, or vice versa. Whether you're picking up your own man or simply whoever is open, get to him quickly and stop him as high on the court as you can; try to keep him from reaching the basket.

Tight defense (above photo) limits the ball-handler's options for both dribbling and passing, because her primary receiver is closely guarded. The receiver on the right can't cut into the lane, so she has to come to the ball-handler for a pass or set a screen.

When caught in a 2-on-1 (left), you should already know who's better at passing, dribbling or shooting so you can decide quickly whether to challenge one player or the other, or stay back for the rebound. If you can pick up the 2-on-1 high, as shown here, so much the better. (Instead of throwing a cross-court pass, the ball-handler should have sent her teammate toward the basket so they could take the play down low, making it tougher on the defensive player.)

If your team misses and the opposition rebounds, one of their players may sprint toward the other basket. If you have the best chance of catching him, don't head straight for the breakaway player; head for the basket at an angle. If you beat him to the basket, you can deny the layup without crashing into his back. If you can stop him higher, there's a 50-50 chance he'll miss an outside shot. Meanwhile, one of your teammates should sprint down the court to be in position for the rebound.

Fast breaks are designed to create overmatches—3-on-2, 3-on-1, 2-on-1—and you may find yourself the lone defender. The offensive players want you to commit to one of them so the others can get open under the basket. Have you studied your opponent so you know who can or cannot shoot or handle the ball? Challenge the poorest ballhandler, stop his dribble, then step back and break up his pass. You take a chance that he'll shoot, but at least he won't be shooting a layup. Don't hesitate to be bold. Breaking up a 2-on-1 or 3-on-1 is not only fun but quite an achievement.

WORK ON YOUR DEFENSE!

Get yourself in top physical and mental condition, and play in pickup games whenever you can. You can improve your defense by playing one-on-one against stronger players, and you can work on dealing with picks and screens by playing 2-on-2 and 3-on-3 with players who know how to set screens and work the "pick and roll." Guard your opponents just as hard in pickup games as you would in a fullscale scrimmage, and you'll find the extra effort paying off for you.

REVIEW

1. Aggressiveness, quickness, preparation, communication and tenacity are the keys to playing winning defense. All these traits can be developed through mental and physical conditioning. Start with tenacity (never giving up!) and the rest will follow.

2. Learn your opponent's moves and tendencies so you're prepared to play smarter defense.

3. Take a comfortable defensive stance in a slight crouch, knees bent, up on the balls of your feet, weight evenly balanced, feet spread about the width of your shoulders.

4. Play defense with two hands and two feet. Always move *both* feet ahead of your body. Use your left hand for steals and blocked shots to mirror a righthanded opponent.

5. Keep your eyes open, your head up, the play always in front of you. Watch your opponent's belt buckle to avoid being easily faked; don't watch the ball, his feet, head or shoulders.

6. Also play your opponent without the ball. Stay between your opponent and the basket and between your opponent and the ball. Learn his favorite shooting spots and beat him to them.

7. Learn to overplay, particularly if you're guarding a player who can only go one way.

8. Learn to sag, switch, press, double-team, and help your teammates.

9. Keep talking on defense at all times. Let your teammates know what's going on and insist that they do likewise, particularly when the offense is setting screens or picks.

10. Never hesitate to call for help when you're overmatched or your opponent breaks away.

11. Take special pride in your defense. Guard the toughest opponent whenever possible. Don't worry about being embarrassed; learn how to adjust against taller and quicker players.

12. Play 1-on-1, 2-on-2, 3-on-3 pickup games to work on your defense as well as your offense!

YOUR DAILY PRACTICE CHECKLIST

__ Run at least five sets of ten wind sprints (40 yards outdoors, or full-court indoors)

__ At least 10 minutes of rapid lateral and backpedaling movement at full speed, 60-second increments, moving both feet with sudden changes of direction

__ Work at least 10 minutes on stretching and agility, as covered in the chapter on conditioning

__ Jumping jacks, trampoline, running the stairs at least 10 minutes total to develop quickness

__ At least a half hour of 1-on-1, 2-on-2, 3-on-3 against the toughest opponent(s) available

REBOUNDING

Rebounding is an integral part of both defense and offense. On defense, you want to allow the other team only one shot. On offense, you want your rebounders fighting for that second, third or fourth shot. A good rebounder is worth his/her weight in gold. If you're a truly superior rebounder, a coach will usually find a place for you in the lineup even if you're not that great a shooter.

Here's an example of how important rebounding is to a team: the Boston Celtic dynasty of the '50s and '60s. The Celtics already had one of the great ballhandlers of all time, Bob Cousy, and a bunch of good shooters. But until they got Bill Russell to get his 20–25 rebounds a game, they never won their division. After they got Russell, they won the championship 11 out of 13 years.

Many people have made a big deal about my averaging a "triple double" (scoring, assists and rebounds) my second season in the NBA and just missing four other times. As a 6'5" guard, how did I average over 10 rebounds a game my first five years? I feel that if you're a fundamentally sound player, rebounding is part of your game at any position. I was a forward in college, and rebounding was part of the job. In the pros, I played a penetrating game, and so did many of the guards I faced. Thus I was often close to the basket on defense. If I was in position for a rebound, I could start the fast break instead of waiting for the outlet pass from a teammate. Your coach will undoubtedly have very definite ideas about the role he or she wants guards to play in rebounding.

THE KEY INGREDIENTS OF REBOUNDING

Rebounding is a very simple proposition. You have to anticipate where the ball will come down, and get to it before anyone else. This takes **(1)** position; **(2)** timing/instinct for the ball; **(3)** strength, to establish and maintain position, and protect the ball once you have it; **(4)** determination, the refusal to be denied when you go for the ball; and **(5)** toughness, or keeping your composure while mixing it up with other players under the board. Rebounding is the most physical part of basketball, and you cannot get rattled or let your emotions take over. You have to focus strictly on going for the ball and not get involved in shoving matches or "getting even" with another player.

Height is helpful, of course, but not unless you know how to get good position and use your height to your advantage. Nor is "vertical leap" helpful in itself. How high you can jump is not nearly as important as *where* you are when you jump (position), or *when* you jump (timing). Tall players especially need to develop leg and upper body strength to be effective rebounders. I can't tell you how many times I've seen a shorter but stronger player swipe a rebound from a taller player.

Often a coach will simply stick his tallest player in the pivot, regardless of athletic ability, and hope the ball falls into that player's hands more often than the other center's. If you're a youngster going through a rapid spurt of growth, and you're called upon to play the pivot, you may feel awkward and uncoordinated. There are exercises to help you develop strength, coordination, flexibility and quickness. If you have the determination to do the extra work, you'll find it pays off.

Timing is the basic instinct for the ball all great rebounders seem to have: where to set up for the rebound, a sense for how the rebound will behave, and a leap with no wasted motion because you're at the peak of your leap as the ball comes off the board. Shorter players who have this gift are said to "play taller." Charles Barkley, who has played forward for years at 6'4," is but one example.

Establishing and maintaining inside position is the key to rebounding. Use your leg and hip strength to get position; keep your hands up so you aren't called for pushing. If you're boxed to the outside, you don't accept that position and concede the rebound; you at least try to set up alongside your opponent. Whether you're inside or outside, you should be able to anticipate from the flight of the ball which way it will rebound, and, keeping your inside position, move in that direction while the ball is in the air.

Determination and toughness are self-explanatory. The ball takes crazy bounces, so you never concede a rebound even if you're boxed out or don't get the ball on your first try. Determination means you keep fighting for the ball as long as it's in play (also known as "second effort" and more). You have to have the discipline to do this without committing stupid fouls (such as pushing off, or making obvious contact while going over the top on a player who has inside position).

You must be tough enough to keep your composure even when play under the basket gets rough. Most of the pushing and shoving may not be seen or called by the officials. Even if an opponent commits a flagrant foul, it's not a good idea to retaliate, because if the official didn't see the foul but sees you retaliate, guess who's going to get the whistle? The better rebounder you are, the more you're going to get hammered under the basket. It's part of the game, like playing a line position in football. You're of more value to your team if you simply concentrate on rebounding. Have your captain or coach complain to the officials and hopefully the calls will eventually even out.

ESTABLISHING POSITION

As a rebounder, your first objective is to get into a position where you're most likely to get the ball: between your opponent and the basket. Any player behind you then either has to reach over you, thus risking a foul, or hope the ball bounces out of your reach. Position enables shorter players to rebound effectively against taller players. Generally a smaller player will be quicker than a taller player and should have the advantage in establishing position. Even if you're small, if you're strong enough to hold onto the ball, you'll get your share of rebounds against taller players.

Quickness and court sense help you get position. For example, if you're a weakside forward on defense (away from the flow of the play), you should automatically head to the basket when the other team is setting up a shot. If the ball rotates back to your side, then your first assignment is to guard your opponent. If you're a guard and you're having trouble with your opponent, you will probably need to face guard that player and keep him outside instead of going for the rebound.

You may not push an opponent or otheWise use your hands to get position; you get position by being quick and alert, and hold your position by using your hip and leg strength. If an opponent gets inside position on you, don't concede; try to squeeze in alongside him. Once you have set your position, that spot should be yours (unless you're a center on offense, in which case you cannot remain in the lane more than three seconds). It's a foul if your opponent pushes to get in front of you or makes contact in reaching over you, although such fouls are not always called.

Establishing position in front of your opponent, between your opponent and the basket, is also known as "boxing out" or "blocking out" under the boards. Sometimes your primary assignment will be to box out an opponent to keep him away from the basket while one of your teammates goes for the rebound. When the rebound is up for grabs, you and your teammates have to let each other know who's going to grab the ball; you don't want to be fighting each other for the rebound.

MOVE TO THE BALL

If your primary assignment is to rebound, your position is not necessarily stationary. You set up between your opponent and the basket so you can *change* position according to the flight of the ball. There's an element of luck to rebounding as well as skill, because a basketball can take crazy bounces; luck, however, tends to favor those who consistently get good position.

If you've devoted enough practice time to rebounding, you've learned to anticipate the direction and distance of the rebound while the ball is still in the air. The force, spin and arch the shooter puts on the ball; the shooter's angle to the basket; and the contact (or lack of contact) the ball makes with the rim or the board, all affect the behavior of the rebound. Rebounders who haven't learned to judge the flight of the rebound simply set up in one spot and hope the ball bounces their way.

Once you've determined where the ball is going, head for that spot and get set for the rebound. You should be relaxed but slightly tensed, like a coiled spring, and completely focused on the ball. You should be planted firmly enough to hold your position, but agile enough to move to the ball and go up for the rebound.

If you have good position, the height of your leap is not as important as timing your leap to meet the ball. Again, with practice this becomes more instinctive. Sometimes the ball hangs on the rim, and sometimes it bounces off harder than you expect. Inside position gives you a better shot at controlling the ball even if you don't grab it cleanly on the first try.

CONTROL AND PROTECT THE BALL

"Two hands for beginners" is a good rule in defensive rebounding. You often see players rebound with one hand, sweeping the ball dramatically off the rim and bringing it down to meet the other hand, or throwing the outlet pass all in one motion. The advantage of one-handed rebounding is that you can jump higher with one arm extended than you can with two. The downside is that it's more difficult to control the ball with one hand, unless you have extraordinarily large hands and considerable arm and wrist strength. Especially if you're rebounding in a crowd, and you usually will be, you can protect the ball better if you control it with two hands. The bottom line is, get the ball by any (legal) means necessary.

Extend yourself fully and grab the rebound with two hands at the peak of your leap. Grip the ball firmly, bring it down and protect it, and decide quickly what you're going to do. **Protect the ball** at the same time as you're looking for a teammate to receive the outlet pass. This means a good grip, ball up in passing position and close to your body, elbows out. Here's why arm and shoulder strength are important. **Use your dribble** to get out of trouble if an opponent challenges you; don't let yourself get tied up. Dribble with the hand farthest from the defender. (This is another reason to master dribbling with either hand.) Keep your head up and call for help from your teammates. If you're double-teamed, that means a teammate is open for a pass.

When you leap for the ball, your fingers should be slightly spread, just as if you were receiving a pass. Once the ball is in your hands, put a lock on it. Grip the ball firmly and bring it down close to your chest, with your elbows extended to protect the ball. This is where upper body strength comes in handy. Pivot away from the other players fighting for the ball and wait for the area to clear out before beginning your dribble or passing the ball upcourt to a teammate.

If you grab a rebound, your opponents are not going to congratulate you and head upcourt; they'll probably swarm you and try to get the ball back. They'll grab your arm, push you off balance, and try to knock the ball out of your grip or tie you up. Use your dribble to get out of trouble, dribbling with the hand farthest from your defender. In the heat of the battle under the boards, too many rebounders forget they have the option of dribbling. They allow an opponent to tie them up or steal the ball, or they force a pass which is intercepted. This is a perfect example of why everyone at every position needs to master dribbling!

GET THE BALL UP THE COURT

Once you've gotten the ball into the clear, find an open teammate and get the ball to that person, unless it's your job to move the ball up the court. First look around to make sure an opponent isn't lurking just out of your line of sight, waiting to cut between you and your teammate and intercept the pass. (Coaches often assign one player to steal the outlet pass whenever possible.) There are probably more careless turnovers after defensive rebounds than in any other phase of the game.

The outlet pass. If you're able to grab an unchallenged rebound on the defensive board, you have an opportunity to look for the outlet pass as you're coming down and get rid of the ball immediately. Rebounding in a crowd, make sure you have control of the ball first. Throwing the outlet pass quickly and accurately is part of a rebounder's job (accurately is more important than quickly). Make sure the receiver sees you, and make sure there isn't an opponent lurking somewhere ready to steal the pass.

If you're double-teamed after you rebound, at least one of your teammates is open. So, as you look upcourt to see how your team is transitioning into its fast break or set offense, you also want to find the teammate who's open closest to you. Ideally, that teammate will come back and help you get the ball out of trouble. Your coach may have a sequence in which he wants you to look for options on the outlet pass, just as a football quarterback has a first read, a second read, and so on.

DENY YOUR OPPONENT THE OFFENSIVE REBOUND

I've just given you a picture of the *ideal* defensive rebound: box out, one leap, grab the ball and pass it upcourt. But things rarely happen the ideal way. Often there's a dogfight for the ball. If you have inside position but didn't get the ball on your first leap, and the ball is still in play, you either have to keep jumping, keep your opponent boxed out so a teammate can go for the rebound, or both. You have two objectives: (1) to deny your opponents the offensive rebound, and (2) to help your team get the ball. Nothing should distract you. This sort of determination, this refusal to be denied the ball, is the stuff of which great rebounders are made.

If you don't have a clear shot at grabbing the defensive rebound, your next best option is to knock the ball away from the play. If you can get even a fingertip on the ball, tip it to a teammate or knock it out of bounds, just so it goes anywhere except to the shooting team.

If an offensive player beats you to the ball, you still may be able to get a hand on it and tip it away so he doesn't get a follow shot. If you can't do this without committing a foul, then play hard defense and try to deny your opponent a shot or pass. Unless you have been instructed by your coach to foul your opponent in a situation like this, try to avoid stupid fouls. Most truly stupid fouls are committed in going for rebounds when the other player already has control of the ball.

KNOW YOUR ROLE IN DEFENSIVE REBOUNDING

Whether or not you go for rebounds will often depend on the role you are expected to play on defense. If you're guarding a good shooter or an opponent who's especially quick, your first assignment will probably be to keep that player away from the basket. Too many defenders forget that assignment. Once the shot is in the air, they take their eyes off the shooter and go after the rebound, only to find that the shooter has slipped around them and come up with the ball. Many an alert shooter has followed his own missed shot for a basket because his defender was lax in blocking him off the boards.

If you're not guarding the shooter, and you're playing close to the basket, or you're on the weak-side, you should instinctively turn for the basket the minute the ball leaves the shooter's hand. At the same time, you still need to make sure you have your opponent blocked away from the boards. You should be between your opponent and the basket as you go for the ball.

If you're a forward or center, you'll be expected to rebound, and to be effective at blocking opponents off the board. (I don't care for the emphasis today on specialization, i.e. power forward vs. small forward— both should be able to rebound.)

If you're a guard, you'll be expected to do your share. Some coaches want their guards to face guard their opponents, keep them outside, and play upcourt for the outlet pass; other coaches allow their guards to roam and play the ball instead of the court. My rule of thumb for a guard is, if you're near the basket and have a clean shot at the rebound, go for it, but don't get caught too far under the basket. Otherwise, you slow down your team's transition game.

OFFENSIVE REBOUNDING

On defense, your objective is to limit your opponent to one shot, control the ball and remove it from the goal. In offensive rebounding, your objective is to keep the ball in play, keep it in the air, until you can score. Thus you not only need to get into position to rebound, but decide in a split second whether to try for a tip-in, take the ball down and pass it to a teammate, or take it down and go back up for a shot yourself.

Next to good position, fingertip control is the most important factor in offensive rebounding. If your hands aren't large enough to control the ball as you tip it with one hand, then you probably shouldn't try for tip-ins; you should bring the ball down with two hands and pass it a teammate who is open for a shot. A good tactic after you've brought the ball down is to fake as if you're going back up; you can often draw a foul this way, or go back up for an uncontested shot.

The secret to successful tip-ins is to get as much of your hand on the ball as possible, controlling the ball with your fingers and wrist just as if you were taking a shot. With your hand controlling the ball, it's easier to guide the ball accurately toward the basket. If you tip the ball only with your fingertips, or slap at the ball with no hand and wrist control, it could go anywhere.

Offensive rebounding requires timing and perseverance (second effort, sometimes third or fourth effort). Often you don't have as good position in offensive rebounding as you do in defensive rebounding. (If your defender has read this book, he or she is already in position, boxing you out.) But even if your opponent has inside position, this doesn't mean you concede the rebound. As long as the ball is in play and not in your opponent's hands, you have as much of a chance to score as they do to get the ball. Keep fighting for the ball (while avoiding stupid fouls) and keep it in play until your team scores or someone takes down the rebound. Each effort becomes more important than the one before. Keep fighting for the ball and wear the other team down!

TIP WITH EITHER HAND!

Your timing on the offensive board will come with practice, just like your instinct for getting to the ball on defensive rebounds. The effort you put into offensive rebounding is a matter of personal determination, also known as work ethic. It can be tiring and frustrating to keep leaping for the ball without getting it, but your efforts will pay off in the long run.

Make it part of your personal practice session each day to work on tip-ins, especially if you're a forward or center. Work with a friend if you can; one person shoots, the other tips. Develop a sense for the angle of the rebound and the angle at which you have to tip it back up. "Knowing all the angles" is important in rebounding at both ends of the court. Skill at tipping the ball will earn you valuable points in games. You also give your opponent a wakeup call when you repeatedly take a second shot at the basket instead of conceding the rebound when your team misses its first shot.

Work on tip-ins with either hand. Whichever side of the basket you're on, it helps to be able to tip with the hand furthest from the basket. You'll have better control of the ball and there will be less chance of having your shot blocked.

Work on tipping off the backboard. A tip-in off the board is usually a better percentage shot than one tipped over the rim. A good rule is: if you're directly in front of the basket, tip over the rim. If you're to either side, tip off the board. It's the same principle as if you were shooting a layup.

As you become more confident at tipping the ball accurately, you might also work on follow shots. A follow shot means you catch the rebound in mid-air and shoot in the same motion, whereas a tip means you guide the rebound back toward the basket. It takes timing, good hands, coordination and concentration to shoot follow shots.

There are times when it's better not to tip the ball or shoot a follow shot. Instead, grab the ball and bring it back down. Often you can fake the defensive player and draw a foul, go back up for an easy basket, or both. A lot of three-point plays result from this simple tactic.

CRASHING THE OFFENSIVE BOARD

Sometimes you may be called upon to "crash" the offensive board: your teammates block out while you go to the hoop. Generally two players block out and a third player crashes. You don't want too many offensive players underneath, because if the other team rebounds, no one's in position to get back on defense. Guards rarely crash the offensive board; you'll generally stay in the backcourt so you can get back quickly on defense, or set up a new play if your team gets the offensive rebound. If you drive for the hoop, beware of getting caught too far under the basket. Make sure you can still get back on defense to pick up your opponent, or switch assignments with a teammate.

If you're called upon to crash the boards, be especially conscious of your hands. You're not supposed to push to get position whether you're on defense or offense, but officials are more likely to call pushing on an offensive player trying to crash the board. Keep your hands no lower than shoulder height and concentrate on the ball and the basket.

Any time you go for an offensive rebound, you're likely to find your path blocked by a defensive player. Unless you're exceptionally tall or a fantastic leaper, you probably can't remain behind that player and still get the rebound. Use your quickness to get inside position (maybe you fake one way and go the other), or try to squeeze in alongside him and use your strength and timing to go up for the ball at the same time he does. Leg strength is extremely important in rebounding, not just for leaping, but for working your way into position and staying there.

Three approaches to offensive rebounding: Above, tipping the ball off the board. You'll generally have better control and accuracy if you use the board (the same principle as shooting a layup). Be able to tip with either hand! Above right, tipping over the rim. Good fingertip and wrist control will give you a more accurate touch. If you slap at the ball or try to tip too hard, you won't have sufficient control. If you can't jump very high or tip accurately, take the ball down with two hands and bank it off the board just as if you were shooting a layup, as the player at right is doing.

As an offensive rebounder, you must exercise restraint and common sense if a defensive rebounder gets the ball. More stupid fouls are committed by offensive players trying to strip the ball from a defensive rebounder than in any other phase of the game. Once a rebounder has full control of the ball, firmly gripped with two hands and protected with his elbows and body, it's foolish to try to take it away; the best thing you can hope for is to tie up the ball without getting called for a foul. You're probably better off getting back on defense, and perhaps going for a steal on the outlet pass. The only time you give a foul in this situation is to prevent a fast break or slow down your opponent's momentum.

Following up an offensive rebound: Instead of tipping the ball, sometimes it's better to rebound it with two hands and pass it to a teammate, or fake your defender and go back up for a shot. This is a good way to draw fouls and add to your scoring opportunities.

PREPARATION AND ANTICIPATION

Preparation plays a large role in rebounding. Before the game, check the baskets. Are the boards metal, wood or glass? The rims tight or loose? What kind of bounce does the ball take off each rim? Each board? If the rims are loose, or "dead," the ball will probably take a shorter bounce than usual. Doing your "homework" in this manner can pay off during the game.

Then, as I've previously noted, you have to be able to anticipate from the flight of the ball which way the rebound is going to go. Generally, a shot which comes in high will rebound to the other side of the rim (a shot from the right side will rebound to the left). If the shot comes in low, it's more likely to rebound to the side from which it was shot. A flat-line shot is anybody's guess.

The amount of spin on the ball will also influence the direction and force of the rebound. The more spin on the shot, the more the rim will deaden the ball so it rebounds in the vicinity of the basket; less spin, and ball is more likely to bounce sharply away from the basket. The more you practice rebounding, the better you'll be able to anticipate the behavior of the ball.

In offensive rebounding, you have an advantage in that the shooter has some idea where the ball is going, so you and your teammates can help each other. If you think your shot is going to fall short, you should yell "Short!" so your teammates can react accordingly. If the ball isn't going to hit anything, yell "Air ball!" so it can be played accordingly. Keep in mind that an air ball does not stop the shot clock.

DEVELOP YOUR REBOUNDING SKILLS

Your timing and instinct for the ball will improve with daily practice. At the same time, you can develop strength, stamina and quickness through physical conditioning. Build your leg and thigh muscles so you can establish and maintain position and jump repeatedly without tiring. Develop your arm and shoulder muscles so you can grab and protect the ball in heavy traffic. Wind sprints and agility drills will help your quickness. Running stairs, skipping rope, jumping jacks and the trampoline can improve your stamina and jumping ability.

If you're serious about becoming a good rebounder, never pass up an opportunity to practice— at home, at the playground, in the gym. If other players are shooting, get under the basket and rebound. Practice tipping the ball, and practice rebounding and passing the ball out to one of the shooters. Sporting goods stores sell devices that cover the basket so the ball always rebounds. Use one of these in private practice to develop your timing. More than anything else, hard work and determination will help you improve as a rebounder.

REVIEW

1. Position, timing, strength, determination and toughness are all more important than height.
2. Quickness helps you get into position and time your leap properly. Leg strength helps you maintain position; upper body strength helps you protect the ball after you grab it.
3. On defense, if you stay between your opponent and the basket as you're supposed to, you'll have the advantage in getting good position for the rebound.
4. If you're guarding the shooter, be sure to block him off the boards before you go to the board.
5. Grab the rebound firmly with two hands and protect it with your elbows and body. Keep your head up and look upcourt for an open teammate.
6. If a teammate is not immediately open, or you're swarmed by the defense, use your dribble to move the ball out of trouble. Dribble with the hand farthest from your defenders.
7. Fingertip control is important in tipping the ball on the offensive board. If you don't have good control of the ball, rebound with two hands so you can shoot or set up a new play.
8. Learn to use the board in tipping. Practice tipping with either hand. The same principles apply to tip-ins as to shooting layups.
9. Avoid stupid fouls! Don't try to strip the ball from a player who has full possession of the rebound; get back quickly on defense and also look for an opportunity to steal the outlet pass.
10. Whether you're on offense or defense, keep fighting for the ball as long as it's in play. Even if you're outjumped the first time, a good second, third or fourth effort could get you the ball.
11. Test the boards and rims before the game to see how they affect the bounce of the ball.
12. Learn to anticipate the direction of the rebound from the angle, arch and spin of the shot while the ball is in the air. Work on rebounding in practice while others are shooting.

YOUR DAILY PRACTICE CHECKLIST:

___ Work on your leap on the trampoline or the court; jump higher than you did yesterday.

___ Wind sprints and agility drills for quickness. Run the stairs for stamina and endurance.

___ Strength conditioning for legs and upper body (perhaps alternate days instead of daily).

___ Grab at least 50 rebounds while other players are shooting.

___ Shoot at least 50 tip-ins (using both the left and right hands) while others are shooting.

DRIBBLING

Dribbling is one of the basic fundamentals of basketball, but I continue to be amazed at how few players at any level truly master it.

Whatever position you play, whatever your size, you must be able to dribble if you want to be a complete basketball player. This means you not only master dribbling with your dominant hand, you dribble at least adequately if not equally well with your other hand. You also know when to dribble and when not to, because dribbling is not the fastest way to move the ball. Passing is.

Dribbling is an integral part of your offensive game, especially in one-on-one situations. It's the basic foundation for setting up shots and creating fakes and moves to the basket. I've seen so many "can't miss" players who could shoot the eyes out of the basket coming off a screen, but could not dribble to create shots for themselves or open up the offense. You also have to be able to dribble to slow down the tempo of the game or give your offense time to set up properly.

Dribbling is also an integral part of the "transition game" from defense to offense. Depending on whether your team has rebounded or inbounded the ball, the transition could result in (1) a fast break, where you want to beat your opponent upcourt for a layup or other high-percentage shot, or (2) your half-court offense, where your team runs designated plays or patterns to set up shots.

Unless you can consistently throw court-length passes with pinpoint accuracy, you'll generally move the ball upcourt in shorter increments by dribbling and passing. If your opponent plays a pressing defense, or double-teams the player with the ball, you have to be a skilled ball-handler who can dribble or pass as the situation demands. If only one player on your team is a good dribbler, your team is in trouble against this type of defense.

The primary reasons for dribbling are (1) to move the ball into scoring position, (2) to create moves to the basket, (3) to get into better position to pass or shoot, (4) to draw out the defense, (5) to allow your offense time to set up, (6) to kill time and eat up the clock, (7) to draw a foul so you can score points or stop play and set up the offense again. In a half-court game, you will probably do less dribbling and more passing, in order to move the ball more quickly.

Today's overemphasis on specialization (point guard or shooting guard, small forward or power forward) has robbed many players of the incentive to master dribbling; they don't feel it's part of their job. And, since practice time is limited, you will not often find coaches spending much time on fundamentals. Dribbling is a skill you will generally have to develop on your own.

WHY FORWARDS AND CENTERS MUST BE ABLE TO DRIBBLE

Guards are not the only players who need to master dribbling. If you're a center or forward who cannot dribble well, you limit your scoring opportunities. The defense can afford to play you tight, cutting down on your options for passing, shooting, receiving the ball, or driving to the basket.

If you're a forward or center who *can* dribble well, you become a real asset to your team. Not only are you more of an individual offensive threat, but you contribute more to the overall offense because you can exchange the ball smoothly with other members of your team. Against a pressing

The key to successful dribbling is fingertip control. You have to "feel" the dribble in your fingertips, hands and wrists so you can dribble without looking at the ball. Your palm should not touch the ball. A hard bounce helps you keep the ball under better control. You can bounce it hard enough to control it and still have "soft hands." It comes with practice. Both players here demonstrate excellent dribbling form. Head up, slight crouch, knees slightly bent, ball low, dribbling hand parallel to the floor, power and control of the ball coming from the wrist and fingertips, body turned slightly to protect the ball from defenders, "off hand" ready to protect the ball.

defense, you become another ball-handler, giving your team more options for defeating the press. Finally, centers and forwards need to be able to dribble after pulling down a defensive rebound so you don't get tied up or have the ball stripped away. You should be able to dribble away from your opponents and out of danger, or advance the ball upcourt before you turn it over to a teammate.

Many tall players are self-conscious about dribbling. They stand erect, bounce the ball too high and move awkwardly. If you stay in a slight crouch and keep your dribble low, you can control the ball better. This is a basic principle of dribbling whatever your height. But your height can also be an advantage. If you keep your body low and your dribble low, and dribble with the hand farthest from the defender, your height alone keeps the defender from getting too close to the ball.

THE BASICS OF DRIBBLING

Dribbling should be a regular part of your daily practice routine. You can and should develop a great deal of skill by working on your own, but you should also constantly test your skill against the best possible competition so you become aware of the areas where you need improvement. These are the basics you need to work on:

1. Control the ball with your fingertips and wrist. The palm of your hand should not touch the ball. Fingertip control is the key to success.

2. Keep your body low and the dribble as low as the situation demands.

3. Dribble without looking at the ball. Keep your head up, your teammates and opponents in view.

4. Dribble equally well with either hand.

5. Master the crossover dribble.

6. Be able to change speeds and directions.

7. Get a good first step.

8. Be able to protect or pass the ball when you're challenged by defenders.

1. CONTROL THE BALL WITH YOUR FINGERTIPS

Dribbling success comes from fingertip control and mastering the relationship between your hand and the ball. Your fingertips and wrists play the key roles in helping you control the ball.

Your fingers should be spread wide enough that only your fingertips touch the ball as you dribble, not the palm of your hand. Your hand should be flat, parallel to the floor, or angled slightly down toward the ball. If your palm is angled up, you will have a tendency to dribble too high and palm the ball, which is a violation.

Your wrist should be flexible, firm but not stiff. Many players make the mistake of dribbling with the entire forearm, keeping the wrist stiff. If you do this, you'll bounce the ball too high, and you won't have it under control. Let your wrist do the work and you'll have better control of the ball. Your forearm is like a rudder, helping you steer the direction of the ball. Your upper arm should be relaxed and close to your body to help you keep the ball close to your body and protect it better.

Your hand should be directly over the center of the ball. Your wrist provides the power as you bounce the ball firmly with your fingertips. You should feel the ball leave and return to your hand without having to look to see where it is. Your hand and fingers should be "soft" and relaxed as the ball bounces back to you. (It's the same principle you use in catching a baseball or football.) Since your hand is firm as you release the ball and soft as the ball returns, you can feel the rhythm of the dribble in your hand.

Beware of dribbling too softly. If you dribble too softly—a "lazy" dribble—an alert defender will be tempted to steal the ball. You want a firm bounce and a good, steady rhythm, which you must also learn to vary to keep the defense off balance. For example, when you're making a move to the basket, you'll generally bounce the ball harder than usual as you take your first step so you can explode past the defender.

When you're dribbling for speed, i.e., in the open court, leading a fast break, driving for the basket, you'll use a higher bounce than if you were more closely guarded. You still want to keep your head up, your eyes scanning the court, the ball under control with your fingertips and wrist, your body forward so your weight is over the ball. Above right, this would be a good illustration of dribbling technique—head up, body crouched, knees bent, ball low, fingertip control—except for two things: you don't want the ball to get too far out in front of you, because it's too easy to steal; and you should have your body angled to protect the ball.

When you look at the ball instead of keeping your head up and watching the defender's eyes, and don't use your body to protect the ball, here's what happens. The defensive player has a clear shot at the ball, unless you can quickly execute a brilliant crossover dribble and go left. You also don't want to dribble to your left using your right hand; that's an open invitation to the defense to steal the ball!

2. KEEP YOUR BODY AND YOUR DRIBBLE LOW

The ideal stance for dribbling is: (1) your knees slightly bent, (2) body relaxed, in a moderate crouch, (3) weight evenly balanced, (4) the ball to the side on which you're dribbling, not out in front of you, (5) your body turned slightly to protect the ball from a defender, (6) head up so you can keep your teammates and opponents in view. I say "moderate" crouch because if you crouch too low, you can cut down your field of vision. Don't get in the habit of standing straight up when you dribble, even when you're wide open, because it's difficult to control the ball in that stance.

If you're closely guarded (defender is within an arm's length), your body should be at an angle to the defender so you can protect the ball, and you should be dribbling with the hand farthest from the defender. Your head should be up; you watch the defender's eyes (which reveal his intentions) as you also constantly scan the court to see where the other players are.

Keep the bounce of the ball low when you dribble, between knee-high and thigh-high. The best way to keep the ball low is to keep your body low, in a moderate crouch. The lower the bounce, the more you're in control of the ball. The defense has less of an opportunity to slap the ball away. With practice, keeping the ball low and in control should become a matter of "muscle memory."

When you're dribbling for speed, in the open court or driving for the basket, you'll use a higher dribble. You still must control the ball with a firm bounce and position your body to prevent it from being knocked away. You also need to work on your exchange, bringing the ball up from a dribble to pass or shoot in one motion; this is when defenders especially like to try for a steal.

3. DRIBBLE WITHOUT LOOKING AT THE BALL

You absolutely must be able to dribble without looking at the ball. If you have to keep looking at the ball, you'll constantly miss shooting and passing opportunities, and opponents will have an easy time coming at you from any direction and batting the ball away.

Your success at dribbling depends not only on your ability to control the ball, but to react quickly to what the defense does. You have to keep your head up so you can keep both the defense and your teammates in full view.

The best athletes are gifted with peripheral vision—the ability to see out of the corners of their eyes. It's like a "sixth sense" in that you can detect motion from one direction while facing another. You can develop some degree of peripheral vision through practice. While you're dribbling with your head up and facing front, your eyes can be scanning the court: ahead, left, ahead, right, ahead.

Many teams build their offense around the fast break, advancing the ball quickly upcourt while transitioning from defense to offense after a rebound or a steal. If you're a guard and on the "point" of the offense, you'll usually be in the center of the court and you must be able to see the action developing to either side while you dribble at full speed. You may also need to execute a perfect pass off your dribble. Obviously you can't be looking at the ball.

If you find it difficult to dribble without looking at the ball, you must practice until the mechanics of dribbling become second nature. Bounce the ball harder to keep from looking at it. As you develop a better feel for the ball and more confidence in your ability, the technique becomes automatic and you can focus on other things at the same time as you dribble. Try these exercises:

(a) Fix your vision on different objects, straight ahead, to the right, to the left, while you dribble. Vary the order in which you look at these objects. Begin by dribbling slowly and then increase your speed. How many times can you bounce the ball with each hand without looking at it? 10? 20? 50? Score yourself and keep track of your improvement each day.

(b) Set up an obstacle course: chairs, traffic cones, stacks of books. Dribble around and between them, righthanded and lefthanded, without looking at the ball. As you become more adept at this, work on changing hands each time you have to change direction to avoid an obstacle.

(c) Wear blinders which make it impossible for you to look down at the ball.

(d) Whenever possible, play with at least two to a side. When you play one-on-one, you have to concentrate on controlling the ball, but it's too easy to fall into the habit of looking at the ball while you dribble because there's only one person guarding you. Learn to sense when someone is trying to steal; learn to pass when double-teamed.

Keep your head up and watch your defender's eyes to anticipate his moves. At left, the dribbler keeps the ball low and can execute a crossover to his left, or fake left and go right. If he continues left dribbling righthanded, the defender has a good chance for a steal.
Dribble with your left hand! Master this one skill and your game takes on a whole new dimension in terms of the shots and moves you can create. With your right foot as the pivot foot, develop a good first step to your left so you can explode past your defender.

The crossover dribble. Keep your head up and watch your defender's eyes, and you'll know when he or she is going to overplay you or try for a steal. That's a good time to change hands. You can fake right before you crossover to the left, but a fake is less critical than good control of the ball. Use a good hard bounce and shift your pivot foot as you change hands, so you can get a good first step.

4. DRIBBLE EQUALLY WELL WITH EITHER HAND

If you can dribble equally well with either hand, you can improve your game 1000%. You gain so many advantages: (1) the defense can't overplay you; (2) you can dribble in any direction with the hand farthest from the defender; (3) you can drive to the basket from either side; (4) you can get open for shots better; (5) you can protect the ball better against double-teams and pressing defenses; (6) you have more options for clearing the ball out after a rebound and moving it upcourt.

You already have the advantage on offense because you know what you intend to do; the defense doesn't. If you can move in only one direction, you give up much of your advantage. When you're dribbling for speed, you'll use your dominant hand most of the time. But if you want to create moves that will get you open for good shots, or if you're the primary ball-handler for your team and often find yourself closely guarded, you'll need to master dribbling with both hands.

To demonstrate what I mean, try moving to your left while dribbling righthanded. See how exposed the ball is? You're practically inviting the defender to steal the ball. You always want to dribble with the hand farthest from the defender. If you were dribbling with your left hand, your body would be between the defender and the ball.

I was able to get open for a lot of jump shots because I could dribble with my left hand. In fact, most of my jumpers came as I was dribbling to my left. This seemed to me to be common sense. The ball was in the hand farthest from the defender, and I was moving away from the defender. Thus the shot was very difficult to block, and I rarely had a jump shot blocked.

5. MASTER THE CROSSOVER DRIBBLE

As you develop confidence in your ability to dribble with either hand without looking at the ball, work on changing your dribble from one hand to the other. This is called a crossover dribble, and it should be a basic part of your offensive repertoire.

Practice the crossover on your own, bouncing the ball back and forth between hands, slowly at first, increasing speed as you feel more in control of the ball. Then work on it while you're being guarded. Keep the ball low and use a good hard bounce. Keep your head up and watch the defender's eyes so you can anticipate his moves and sense the best time to change hands. If you have to look at the ball, your defender may cut off the direction you had intended to go, or steal the ball.

The crossover is an extremely valuable move because it gives you so many different options. Three are shown here: continue your drive to the left; "cross back" to the right; or, once you've got your defender backpedaling, stop and go up for a shot.

Forget about the fancy crossovers! The showboating, behind-the-back or between-the-legs dribble. Save these until you have absolutely mastered the basics of the crossover. You use the hotdog moves only when nothing else will work. Too many youngsters practice only the fancy moves and neglect the basics. Precise execution of the basic moves is more important. The crossover dribble is one of the most basic moves of the game, and yet so few players become really skilled at it.

6. BE ABLE TO CHANGE SPEEDS AND DIRECTIONS

An important part of your practice routine should be changing speeds as you dribble—half speed, three quarters, full speed—changing directions, creating moves off the dribble, and passing off the dribble. Your objective is to be able to change speeds and directions in a split second. Whatever your speed and the height of your dribble, keep your head up and the ball under control.

By varying the speed and height of your dribble, you can lull the defender into believing you're slowing down or speeding up. We react to sights and sounds unconsciously without intending to. You can dribble on the move, stop and dribble in place for a second, and then start again at a faster pace, ideally with a loud, hard bounce. This is called the "stop and go," and it's a basic move. If you can add a crossover off the stop and go, that gives you two moves instead of one.

If you dribble at a steady pace, stay in a slight crouch and keep the ball low, you'll find it easier to change speeds or execute fakes. Be sure you have the ball under control before you change speeds. It's embarrassing to fake out a defender but neglect to bring the ball with you. Before you execute a fake, you should know where everyone is on the court and know what your other options are in case your move doesn't work out as planned.

Also work on passing off the dribble. Some coaches are opposed to passing off the dribble; they want you to come to a complete stop first. I feel that being able to pass off the dribble helps you move the ball quicker, keeps the defense off balance and adds more options to your offensive game.

For example, if you can throw an accurate one-handed bounce pass off the dribble, you can get the ball to a teammate much faster than if you come to a stop first. If you're in a crouch, you'll be able to bounce the pass more accurately. In the open court, dribbling at a higher speed—for example, on a fast break—you'll generally bring the ball up for a chest pass. You have to make the exchange from dribble to pass within one and a half steps to avoid a traveling violation.

Get a good first step. If you can dribble with either hand, you can move in any direction. Whichever hand you're dribbling with, getting a good long first step is the key to driving for the hoop, driving your defender into a pick, or creating a move away from your defender to get open for a shot. Remember the wind sprints and the hamstring stretch we discussed in the chapter on Conditioning? Here's where they pay off. Push off your pivot foot with as long a stride as you can and explode past your defender.

7. GET A GOOD FIRST STEP

If you're dribbling with your right hand, your left foot is your pivot foot. You should be able to step in any direction with your right foot—forward, backward, to one side or the other—and push off on your left foot. If you're dribbling lefthanded, your right foot is your pivot foot and you stride with your left foot. If you're in a moderate crouch as you dribble, you'll find you can take a longer stride and step off quicker and with more body control.

As you dribble, practice taking short, medium and long steps, forward, back, to either side. This is how you develop a "move" off the dribble. For example, a short step forward, a short step back, a long step forward and gone! If you can dribble with either hand, you've doubled the number of moves available to you.

If you've built up your legs and your quickness with exercises and wind sprints, you'll find it much easier to get a good first step. You should literally explode off your back foot so that even if your defender reacts immediately and moves both feet as he should, you're past him before he can recover. I had enough confidence in my quickness and my dribbling technique that I felt I could beat anyone with a fake and a good first step.

8. PROTECT THE BALL WHEN YOU'RE CHALLENGED

Many players lack confidence in their dribbling skill, so they stop dribbling when challenged by a defender. Once you've stopped, you can't resume dribbling unless a defender knocks the ball out of your hands, so you either have to hold the ball or give it up. A clever defensive player will often fake a steal, then step back to cut off the pass when you stop your dribble.

You don't want to stop your dribble too high. Use your body and your "off" hand to protect the ball until a teammate comes to you for a pass (taller players should have less trouble getting open) or sets a pick. Once the defense knows you'll stop, they'll stop you higher and higher up the court.

When you're challenged by a defender, use your body and your "off" hand to protect the ball, as shown in the photo at left. Keep your head up and watch the defender's eyes. At the same time, use your peripheral vision to see where everyone else is on the court. At right, some common mistakes: turning your back on the defender; dribbling too high; looking at the ball instead of keeping your head up. When a defender tries to turn you, you have to attack the defender with a move that gives you the advantage; for example, a crossover dribble, a reverse pivot, a stop and start. You should also be looking for an open teammate to whom you can pass.

When you're challenged, keep your head up and attack the defender instead of tensing up and reacting. What angle is the defender coming from? A stop-and-go or a crossover the other way should beat him. Are his hands held high? You may be able to dribble past him. If they're low, he has a better chance for a steal and you may need to pass. Is his weight forward or back? Forward, you can step back to make him commit, then change speeds or direction and drive around him. If he's back on his heels, you should be able to beat him with a good first step in either direction.

If a defender is taller or quicker than you, and has successfully challenged your dribble or passes, you may not want to attack him one-on-one; you'll probably need help from your teammates. If the defender is guarding you closely, a good way to shake loose is to force him into a screen set by one of your teammates, which could also set up a pick-and-roll for an easy basket.

Don't let a defender turn you. This is another common mistake. Only a center plays with his back to the basket. When you turn your back, you can't see which teammates are open, and you eat up time dribbling instead of passing. You're also more vulnerable to a double-team or a steal.

It's OK to turn your back momentarily, but unless you're deliberately killing time, you should then be prepared to pass, or shake loose from your defender with a reverse pivot and turn back facing the basket in the other direction. I'm not necessarily the best example here, because I turned my back a lot. It was part of my game because I liked to post up a defender and back him down toward the basket. I'd also usually draw a double-team and that would open up one of my teammates.

DRIBBLING AGAINST A DOUBLE-TEAM

Players often look at the ball while dribbling because they're afraid of it being stolen. In reality, whenever you look at the ball, you're not only tying up your team's offense, you're inviting the defense to double-team you. In a typical double-team, a second defender comes from your blind side and tries for a steal. Double-teaming is part of the game, so you have to learn how to deal with it. First, try to pass the ball to an open teammate. If you're double-teamed, someone else has to be open. If you're guarded too closely or a teammate isn't within passing range, however, don't force the pass; you have to have enough confidence in your dribbling ability to dribble out of trouble.

If you try to dribble between two defenders, at least one of them will have a clear shot at the ball. And you can't barrel through the double-team like a fullback hitting the line, because you could get called for an offensive foul. In fact, part of the strategy involved in double-teaming is to try to draw you into a charging foul. Instead, dribble parallel to the defenders without turning your back. Use a stutter step (stop and go) or a crossover dribble to shake loose. Call for a teammate to set a pick or come to you for a pass. Keep your cool and enjoy the challenge of beating the double-team.

If a teammate is dribbling and you see a double-team developing, not only should you warn him, but you should be prepared to move quickly into position to receive a pass from him.

REVIEW

Practice dribbling on your own and with someone guarding you. Work on developing "muscle memory" and good habits. If you've developed bad habits, practice until you've corrected them.

1. Keep your body in a slight crouch, knees bent, weight evenly distributed, head up.
2. Your hand should be flat, parallel to the floor, or angled downward. Your palm should not come into contact with the ball. Dribble with your wrist and fingertips.
3. Control the ball with your fingertips. "Feel" the ball as it leaves and returns to your hand.
4. Keep the ball low and bounce it firmly. A lazy bounce is easier to steal.
5. Dribble without looking at the ball. A harder bounce will help.
6. Keep your head up and watch your defender's eyes. Scan the court to keep teammates and opponents in view at all times.
7. Keep your body between the ball and the defender. Use your "off" hand to keep the defender at arm's length. Dribble with the hand farthest from the defender.
8. Master dribbling equally well with each hand. Do not be satisfied with anything less.
9. Always get a good first step by pushing off your rear (pivot) foot. Use your dribble to create fakes, moves and opportunities for shots. Learn to pass off the dribble.
10. Master the crossover dribble. Work on changing speeds and directions while you dribble.
11. Avoid the fancy stuff (behind the back, between the legs) until you have mastered the basics.
12. When a defender challenges you, attack the defender instead of stopping your dribble.
13. Avoid turning your back on a defender. Develop the moves necessary to get past him.
14. Learn how to pass and dribble against a double-team while avoiding the offensive foul.
15. Know when to stop dribbling and pass the ball.

YOUR DAILY PRACTICE CHECKLIST:

___ Set up an "obstacle course" and dribble through it with each hand, without looking at the ball.

___ Work on your first step and dribble to your right using your right hand, left using left hand.

___ Work on your crossover dribble and crossback dribble in each direction.

___ Dribble the length of the court at full speed using each hand.

___ Work on stop-and-go and changing speeds.

___ Work with teammates on creating bounce passes and chest passes off the dribble.

___ Work on creating moves to the basket off the dribble: driving the lane using each hand, driving the baseline from either side.

___ Work on your reverse pivot and double reverse pivot while dribbling, starting from various spots on the court.

PASSING

Passing is the quickest way to move the ball. Dribbling might be safer if the dribbler is skilled at protecting the ball, but it eats up more time. The best ball-handlers can dribble and pass equally well, and know when to do which.

Good passing requires constant practice. As you get to know your teammates, your pass release will become quicker, your passes more accurate. Good passing looks easy, but it is a precise art. Sloppy passing results in turnovers and missed opportunities. Good passing leads to baskets.

Centers and forwards may be able to get by without being expert dribblers, but everyone on a team must be able to pass. In particular, a center who plays facing away from the basket must be able to pass well in all directions. A rebounder must be able to throw the "outlet" pass after getting the rebound. This is a vital part of the "transition game."

Every team needs at least one playmaker, a skillful passer who can get the ball to other players in scoring position. (Ideally, each player should be able to do this.) An outstanding passer who can also shoot reasonably well will always have a place in basketball, regardless of his or her size. An outstanding passer can be worth 20–40 points a game to his or her team.

I always knew I could score, and I wanted the ball when the game was on the line. But I got even more enjoyment out of threading the needle with a perfect pass to set up a basket by one of my teammates. The more everyone was involved in the offense, the better chance we had of winning. Regardless of how many points I scored, I also wanted a bunch of assists (a pass that leads directly to a field goal). I took pride in leading the NBA in assists 8 of the 14 years I played, and holding the alltime record for total assists until it was broken by Magic Johnson in 1991.

PASSING CREATES SCORING OPPORTUNITIES

If you've ever played in a game where you were consistently open but never got to shoot because a "gunner" wouldn't give up the ball, perhaps you developed more of an appreciation for passing.

Passing is not an either-or proposition, as in either you pass or you shoot. Passing does not reduce your scoring opportunities. Passing *creates* scoring opportunities for everyone including the passer.

First of all, defenders have a tendency to play back from a player who's a passing threat, whereas they will usually play closer to a player who tends to dribble a lot. When the defender stays back, the player with the ball has more opportunities to shoot.

Second, you have to pass to keep the offense moving. A well-designed offense creates mismatches (tall player vs. short, quick player vs. slow) and it creates open shots under the basket. Good, crisp passing creates the flow of movement that sets up these scoring opportunities. If you're part of that flow, you'll often find yourself open near the basket to take a return pass from a teammate.

If you can dribble and pass equally well, and you're not afraid to go to the hoop, you will create numerous scoring opportunities. If you can consistently beat single coverage defense, you should

Fingertip control is critical in passing, just as in shooting and dribbling. Hold the ball firmly but not too tight, evenly balanced in your hands, fingers along the seams if possible. Take a step (so you can get your body behind the ball), snap your wrists, release the ball off your fingertips at least a forearm's length from your body, and follow through. The snap puts a spin on the ball which makes the pass more accurate. Don't shove the ball with your wrists stiff. You have little control of the ball that way.

The chest pass is the pass you'll use most often. Step, snap your wrists and release the ball off your fingertips with a good follow-through, as shown at right. You want to work on getting this pass off quickly while maintaining accuracy, hitting the receiver about chest or shoulder-high.

be able to drive for layups or draw fouls. Layups and free throws go up on the scoreboard with the same value as jump shots. If you draw double coverage, then a teammate is open for a shot.

A smart passer keeps everyone involved in the game, and is always looking for an edge. Let's say a teammate is guarded by a key opponent who's in foul trouble. You pass to that teammate, who draws a foul and the opponent sits down. Or when a teammate blocks a shot, grabs a key rebound or steals the ball, you get the ball back to that person at the other end of the court so he or she can score. If you keep the ball moving with passes and everyone gets to touch the ball, you'll usually find that everyone plays just a little harder simply because they do feel more involved.

GOOD PASSING IS AT THE CORE OF PLAYING AS A TEAM

The best way for a team to score is to get the ball to a player who is open underneath the basket, or otherwise open for a high percentage shot.

If you can help your team win by passing to teammates who are consistently in better position to score, or who are simply better shooters, then that's the role you should be prepared to play. Too many players think only of themselves. It's easy to get disgusted when a teammate shoots all the time and never passes; it's human nature to want to take a shot when you finally get the ball. But if you think like a winner, you focus on team success instead of individual glory.

Few coaches will discourage you from shooting when you have a high-percentage shot. But they generally want everyone to take a quick look first to see if a teammate is open for an even higher-percentage shot. If you take too many bad shots instead of passing off, or you take good shots when teammates are open for even better shots, the coach may invite you to sit down.

You cannot practice passing too much. For one thing, much of the same "muscle memory" you develop in learning to pass accurately will also work to your benefit in shooting. Second, more passing in practice should cut down on the number of turnovers in a game. Hopefully your coach runs plenty of passing drills. Whether or not this is so, you'll benefit from putting in extra time to work with teammates on your own. In football, passers devote hours to timing each receiver's speed, learning his fakes and moves, learning which routes he runs best, and throwing to spots.

As with dribbling and shooting, passing is a matter of fingertip control. The fingers, wrists and arms are all involved in the execution of a properly-thrown pass. Your palms should not touch the ball. As the pass leaves your hands, you should be able to feel in your fingers whether it's on target.

In passing, you often have to get rid of the ball in the blink of an eye, and you'll use your upper arm and shoulder muscles more than in dribbling. Upper body strength helps you put the proper amount of force behind your passes. You can't afford to let your arms get tired as the game goes on.

You also need to work on receiving passes as well as throwing them. A pass should be caught with the hands, not the body. Your hands should be "soft," that is, fingers relaxed and spread naturally. Don't tense your hands or fight the ball as it comes to you; let it come into your hands and then grip it. Catch it with your fingers, not your palms.

You have to be totally focused on the ball. A pass does not always travel in a straight line; it may rise or drop, and break to the right or left. You have to read the spin on each of your teammates' passes and "play the ball." Every pass will not be perfectly thrown, so you have to judge the flight of the ball and move as necessary to catch it at the right level; you can't wait until the ball is upon you and then move. The exception might be a bounce pass thrown too close to your feet, in which case, if there's room, you may step back so the ball reaches your hands at a higher level.

Set a target for the passer whenever possible. A pass at chest or shoulder height should enable you to bring the ball into shooting position, get off a pass or begin your dribble all in one motion. Be prepared to move to the ball instead of standing still. You might also want to fake in one direction to throw the defender off balance before you come back and set your target.

Keep the defense off-balance with a fake in one direction before you pass in another. Don't let yourself get predictable by always passing in the same direction. The passer demonstrates a good step, wrist snap and fingertip release. Ideally, on a pass to the left you'd want to step with your left foot, but in this case the left foot has already been established as the pivot foot. The defensive player, by the way, is making the passer's job easier by keeping her legs straight and moving only one foot at a time instead of both feet.

The "right level" for a pass is one where you can catch the ball and go on to pass, dribble or shoot in one motion. This is generally about chest-high, although some players like the ball even higher for shooting. I always wanted to know the level at which each of my teammates preferred to catch the ball so I could get it to them at that point.

BASIC PASSING TECHNIQUE: STEP, SNAP AND FOLLOW THROUGH

Your fingers should be spread naturally, as wide as necessary for you to control the ball with your fingertips. Wherever you hold the ball in relation to your body, you want to pass the ball by snapping your wrists. Do not pass with your wrists stiff, or shove the ball with your forearms, because you will not have good control of the ball. Snapping your wrists puts a spin on the ball and sends it on a more accurate path toward your target.

Your hands should be along the sides of the ball, fingers fully extended along the seams and spread comfortably. Whether you're upright or in a slight crouch, create a mental picture of your target, take one step toward the receiver and snap the ball off your fingertips at a point in front of your body roughly the length of your forearms. If you release the pass too close to, or too far from, your body, you won't get enough force on the ball. Follow through on the pass by extending your arms.

As the step, snap and follow-through motion becomes a matter of "muscle memory," then you should begin to work on releasing the ball quicker while still maintaining accuracy. You may be able to pass accurately at one speed in practice, but in a game, the speed of play and the level of intensity get cranked up a notch or two. In game situations, particularly when the clock is a factor, you want to release the ball quickly, but without hurrying the pass.

There are two-hand passes and one-hand passes. Both must be thrown with good technique and the ball in complete control. For that reason, I encourage younger players to stick with two-hand passes because their hands aren't always large enough to control the ball with one hand. You should master as many different types of passes as you can, because each one is useful in certain situations. The mark of a complete player is your ability to adjust to any situation.

A bounce pass (left) one handed or two, should bounce at least halfway to the receiver, and reach the receiver about waist-high. Make sure you put enough muscle behind this pass because the floor slows down the ball. Passing from a slight crouch helps you get more of your weight behind the ball. Work on this pass with your teammates in practice to get a feel for the ball and the court.

Leading the receiver (top photo). You'll often lead a teammate with a bounce pass as he cuts toward the basket. You want the ball to wind up at least waist-high at a spot where your teammate can receive it without breaking stride. If the ball bounces too low, behind, or too far in front of your teammate, you risk a turnover. Practice this pass with different teammates because they'll vary in height and each will move toward the basket at a different speed.

THE CHEST PASS

The pass you'll use most often is the chest pass. Snap it off with two hands about a forearm's length in front of your chest, and the pass should reach the receiver at about the same level. If you aim for your teammate's shoulders, the ball should wind up at about his chest, which is usually the preferred receiving position. If he's going to shoot, he can quickly bring the ball into shooting position, and if he's going to pass, the ball will already be in passing position.

Put enough force on the pass so your teammate doesn't have to come back toward you for the ball. Your step, snap and follow-through should give you just the right amount of force, control and accuracy. Many players pass the ball too softly, and their passes get intercepted. The force of the pass, of course, depends on how close you are to the receiver. Practice will help you judge the amount of force you need to put on the ball in relation to the distance you have to cover.

If you're practicing on your own, hang a target—a basketball jersey would be good— about the height of your own chest and another about the height of your waist, and pass from various angles and distances. (The waist-high target is for bounce passes, which I'll get to in a minute.) Garage doors, barn doors and gym walls are good places to hang targets. Or hang a tire from a tree limb and use it as a target, just as you would for football or baseball. Location is just as important in passing as distance, so work on passing accurately to spots. Once you can hit your target consistently (10, 15, 20 in a row) from one angle, then change the angle or increase your distance.

Keep working on the chest pass until it becomes second nature. Start your practice routine each day with chest passes at various distances before you even begin shooting, passing to both sides as well as straight ahead. Righthanded players tend to pass to the right, lefthanders to the left. You do not want your passing pattern to become predictable. Smart defensive players will learn your habits quickly and intercept your passes.

Leading the receiver: Here's a good illustration of how to lead a receiver properly in a pick-and-roll situation. The pass reaches the receiver at a point where he can catch the ball and shoot a layup in one step without breaking stride.

As you become more accustomed to passing from a standing position, you can begin working on throwing the chest pass off the dribble or on the run, as you would in such open-court situations as a fast break.

Passing while moving presents a challenge, particularly when you have to catch the ball and pass it in one motion. You may not always have the release point you want, and you may not be able to grip the ball exactly as you'd like, but you still have to snap your wrists and pass with force and accuracy. There may even be times when you're moving away from your target as you pass. Accuracy is your foremost consideration. Never force a pass just to get rid of the ball.

THE TWO-HAND BOUNCE PASS

A second fundamental pass is the two-hand bounce pass. This pass may be used to bring the ball upcourt, hit the lead man on a fast break, start a play in the half-court game, or hit a teammate cutting to the basket. You must be able to throw this pass to your left, right or straight ahead, and you often have to hit a fast-moving target.

While the chest pass is usually thrown from a more upright position, the two-hand bounce pass is best thrown from a slight crouch, and sometimes off the dribble. The crouch helps you get more of your body behind the ball. Your release point will generally be about waist-high; otherwise, the same step, snap and follow-through apply as with the chest pass. With a bounce pass, you have two targets: the receiver, and a second, invisible target, the spot on the court where you're going to bounce the ball. You don't look at the floor target, you "sense" it as you bounce the ball.

Generally, you want to bounce the ball at least halfway between you and the receiver. However, the court surface, the composition of the ball and its air pressure—hopefully yours is properly inflated and takes a true bounce—also come into play. Rubber and leather balls take different bounces on different surfaces—hardwood courts (permanent and temporary), concrete, asphalt, grass. Even in the best arenas, you find dead spots on temporary floors. The parquet floor at the old Boston Gardens was notorious for this. So you have to check out the court.

Since the bounce slows down the velocity of the pass, you have to put enough force on the ball so the pass doesn't die before it reaches the receiver. The force comes not just from arm and shoulder strength, but from your wrist snap and follow-through.

When you throw the two-hand bounce pass to a teammate cutting to the basket, you "lead" him; that is, you pass to the spot where he'll catch the ball instead of the spot where he's standing when you start the pass. You must be able to gauge your teammate's speed, otherwise the ball winds up behind or too far ahead of him and you have a turnover. This is why passing drills are important.

You want a bounce pass to reach your teammate slightly above the waist. However, it's better for the pass to reach him too high than too low, because a high bounce is easier to handle. If the pass is too low, your teammate may lose momentum or balance. If he's cutting to the basket, you don't want him to have to stop and wait for the ball, stoop for the ball, or have to come back for the ball. You also don't want to throw the ball too hard for the receiver to handle.

Practicing bounce passes with a waist-high target is helpful if you're practicing by yourself, and practicing with a teammate is even better.

When should you use the bounce pass and when should you use the chest pass? As a general rule, the chest pass is your better bet unless the defender is in a position to stop it. If you throw it properly, you should have better control of this pass than any other. Other factors to take into account: Is your opponent playing man-to-man or zone? If man-to-man, how quick and how close is the player guarding the intended receiver? You should always try to pass away from the defender. Where are the defender's arms? Up, a bounce pass may work better; down, a chest pass.

THE ONE-HAND BOUNCE PASS

This is a good pass to use when you're closely guarded and can't bring the ball into position for a chest pass or two-hand bounce pass. Whether you're stationary or dribbling, throw this pass from a slight crouch in a single, fluid motion. In dribbling, your hand is over the ball. To throw the one-hand bounce pass, your hand is behind the ball to give the pass sufficient force and accuracy. You step, snap and follow through just as you would with any other type of pass.

You can also throw long one-hand bounce passes to move the ball up the court quickly, using more of an overhand (baseball pitcher) motion, which will help you put more force behind the ball than you normally get on a two-hand bounce pass. Work on this pass in practice and make sure you have it down cold before you try it in a game. Again, check the court to see how the ball bounces.

One-hand bounce pass: You should be able to throw this pass from a stationary position or off the dribble. Practice releasing the ball quickly, accurately and with just the right amount of force. In your pregame drill, check out the court surface so you know what kind of a bounce the ball is going to take, and adjust accordingly.

The overhead pass is useful in a variety of situations, particularly passing into the pivot. Do not grip the ball too tightly or pass with stiff wrists; you'll lose the spin and the ball will sail. Snap your wrists and release the ball off your fingertips just as with other passes. Your teammate should give you a target; adjust the force of the pass to the distance you have to cover. Your teammate should also be prepared to move toward the ball.

THE OVERHEAD PASS

The overhead pass is thrown with two hands and can be used to get the ball to a player in the pivot (who will usually have his back to the basket), to a tall player face guarded by a shorter player, or as a lob pass to a teammate cutting to the basket. Sometimes you aim it upward, sometimes downward. Forwards and centers have to be just as adept at throwing this pass as guards.

The overhead pass is thrown with a snap of the wrists, but with perhaps just a bit less spin than you'd put on a chest pass or bounce pass. Your release point could be just above your head or higher. This pass is best thrown from moderate distances—10 to 15 feet—although some players like to fling long overhead passes cross-court (the kind that make coaches cringe). As a rule, the harder you throw this pass, the less control you'll have.

An overhead pass should not be intercepted if executed properly. You're going to throw it over the head of the person defending you, and the receiver should be between you and the defender. You have to throw the ball hard enough to reach your teammate, but not so hard that your teammate can't handle the ball. You need a good touch combined with accuracy and a quick release. Certain players will throw this pass better than others, so you may want to use two or three passes to get the ball to your best passer, who then gets the ball to the final receiver.

If you're passing into the pivot, the defender will generally be overplaying to one side or the other, with a hand in front of your teammate. Your teammate should give you a target with one or both hands to indicate where he wants the pass: shoulder-high, head-high, overhead. You have to pass to your teammate's target and far enough away from the defender's hands to keep the pass from being intercepted or batted away. The receiver has to be prepared to move to the ball.

The hook pass comes in handy when you're closely guarded and a chest or bounce pass would be unsafe. Spin the ball off your fingertips with the same motion as if you were shooting a hook shot. While you want a good spin on the ball, getting this pass off quickly, accurately and with sufficient force are more important. Work on throwing the hook pass while you're moving toward the basket.

THE HOOK PASS

This pass is thrown with the same motion as a hook shot except that you aim downward toward the receiver's hands instead of up toward the basket. You want the ball to reach your teammate about chest or shoulder-high, and you want to be able to throw the hook pass with either hand. To throw this pass accurately, you need fingertip control, just as you do in shooting.

The hook pass can be useful in getting the ball into the pivot from a forward position, and vice versa. It can also be used quite effectively when you're driving to the basket and find yourself double-teamed, or you're in a 2-on-1 or 3-on-2 fast break situation. You can hook the ball over the head of a defender to an open teammate, or flip it back to a teammate who is trailing the fast break.

I do not recommend trying the hook pass against a taller or more agile defender. It's pretty hard to throw this pass without tipping off your intentions, and if a defender knows what is coming, he can react accordingly.

THE UNDERHAND PASS

The underhand or "shovel" pass is useful in tight situations where there's too much of a crowd to risk either a chest pass or a bounce pass. If your defender is playing you tight with his hands up, and your target receiver is also tightly covered, the underhand pass can be ideal. This pass should be used only at close range, and works best if the receiver comes to the ball. It's not so much a pass as a quick toss, like a short pitchout in football.

A pivotman will often toss an underhand pass to a teammate cutting off the high post or a screen the pivotman has set up elsewhere. You can also use this pass to get the ball out of a crowd after a defensive rebound.

Even though you're bringing the ball up underhanded, make sure you control the ball with your fingers. Putting a spin on this type of pass isn't as critical as tossing it to the right spot for the receiver to grab it on the run, somewhere between waist - and chest-high. I recommend using two hands whenever possible; one hand is okay as long as you have the ball under control.

The underhand pass (above) is useful at short range when you're closely guarded and a teammate has to come to you for the ball. It's like a short toss in football. Flip the ball up to the spot where your teammate can grab it on the run at waist or chest level. Make sure you've protected the ball up to the time you release it.

The lob pass (right) is useful when you're closely face guarded and a straight pass is likely to be intercepted. For example, an inbounds pass, or, as shown here, a pass into the pivot. Release the pass with the same motion as a two-hand set shot, and aim for the spot where the receiver should catch the ball. This pass is often thrown to a center or forward cutting toward the basket.

THE LOB PASS

The lob pass is more like a shot, the difference being that your target is not the basket, but the spot where a teammate will be. You have to put a good arch and spin on the ball just as if you were shooting a two-hand set shot (which hardly anyone shoots any more) and get it to a precise spot.

The three most common situations where you'll use the lob pass are (1) inbounding the ball, especially when you're closely guarded; (2) getting the ball into the pivot over the hands of a defender who's taller than you; and (3) leading a teammate who's cutting toward the basket.

We used to call this the "alley oop" pass, after it was so named by a San Francisco 49ers football receiver named R.C. Owens. His quarterback would lob the ball toward a spot in the end zone and R.C. would pull it down with a spectacular leap. As faster and more agile big men started coming into the NBA, a passer could lob the ball toward the basket with the same motion as a shot, and the receiver could grab the ball in mid-air and stuff it into the basket. Players who couldn't get up quite that high could still catch a lob pass and continue on for a layup without breaking stride.

The lob pass is a "timing" pass, so obviously you have to practice it with your teammates to get your timing down in each of the three situations described above. The ability of the receiver to get to the ball is as critical as the touch the passer puts on the ball.

The baseball pass (left) is actually thrown more like a football, with a release point behind your ear. Get your body into the pass with a good step and follow through for accuracy. In practice, see how much spin you get on the ball and adjust accordingly, because this pass doesn't always travel in a straight line. You'll often be leading your receiver as opposed to passing to a stationary target.

The sidearm pass: A sidearm or three-quarter overhand pass can give you good distance, but this type of delivery can also put a reverse spin on the ball. See how your pass behaves at long distances in practice before you try it in game situations.

LONG ONE-HAND PASSES

Two other passes you can use, primarily in full-court situations, are long overhand and sidearm passes. These passes take practice to throw precisely, and I do not recommend that you spend time working on them until you've mastered the more basic passes covered earlier in this chapter, and then only if your hand is large enough to control the ball properly.

The overhand pass, also known as the baseball pass, is often used as an outlet pass after a rebound, or an inbound pass when time is precious. It is actually thrown with a delivery more similar to a football pass in that the best release point is behind your ear. You have to step toward your target to get your body behind the ball, and follow through for accuracy. You need sufficient arm strength to reach your target with enough force, otherwise you run the risk of an interception. At the same time you have to be careful of overthrowing the ball, because the ball will sail when you throw it long distances.

The sidearm pass is thrown just as it sounds, by whipping the ball around your body sidearm. This type of pass is also used for outlet passes and long inbounds passes. The good news is that you can generally get more force behind a sidearm pass than an overhand pass. The bad news is that the farther you throw a sidearm pass, the more reverse spin there is on the ball, and for that reason it can be difficult to throw accurately.

A good rule of thumb is, the longer the pass, the more time a defensive player has to get to it. If you're going to throw either pass in a game, you should master it in practice first, working with your receivers to lead them accurately. These passes look spectacular when you throw them, but they can also lead to turnovers unless you can throw them precisely at long distances.

The outlet pass: After you've pulled down a defensive rebound, you'll generally get the ball upcourt with an outlet pass. You can use whatever type of pass you can throw accurately in that particular situation. Do not hurry the pass just to get rid of the ball; use your dribble if necessary. Turnovers happen in this situation because the rebounder threw a wild pass, or didn't scan the court first to make sure an opponent wasn't lurking out of his line of sight to go for an interception. Make the pass upcourt instead of across the court.

When not to pass: The photo at right shows you a good example. Your defender is laying back for a pass, your receiver is 20 feet away and closely guarded. In a situation like this, use your dribble to get closer if you have a dribble; have your teammate come to you; or pass into the corner if the forward is open and let him pass the ball into the pivot. Or, the pivotman may be able to reverse toward the basket and you can lob the ball to him.

HOW TO AVOID PASSING TURNOVERS

Passes result in turnovers for a variety of reasons:

- They are thrown too hard or too softly
- They are thrown carelessly, not accurately enough
- The passer does not have the ball under control
- The passer does not get rid of the ball quickly enough
- The passer chooses a type of pass that is not appropriate for the situation
- The passer "telegraphs" where the ball is going
- The passer tries to force the pass into a crowd, or to a teammate who's too closely guarded
- The receiver for whom the pass is intended is not paying attention
- The individual passer's habits or the team's offense is too predictable

You have to work on passing quickly, accurately and without revealing your intentions to the defense. The easiest ways to help the defense are to look directly at the target of your pass, to step off toward your receiver too slowly, or always to begin a play by passing in the same direction.

When you're running set plays within the context of your team's offense, you'll know the patterns and capabilities of your teammates. If you're freelancing, which is generally the case in pickup games, you have to be a quick study of everyone's capabilities and tendencies on both offense and defense. For example, if a certain defender always goes for the steal, you can make him commit with a fake pass and then get the ball to the open player.

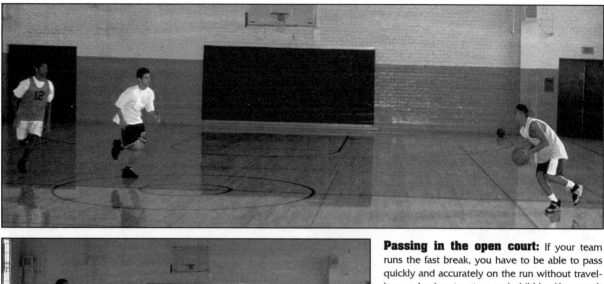

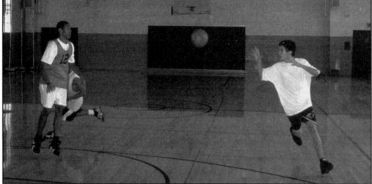

Passing in the open court: If your team runs the fast break, you have to be able to pass quickly and accurately on the run without traveling or having to stop and dribble. You won't always be able to catch the ball exactly where you'd prefer it, or grip the seams exactly as you'd like, but you still have to get off good passes. You have to lead your teammates with passes which are precisely on the spot, neither behind nor too far ahead of them. You have to keep the entire court in your field of vision and remain alert for defenders who may try to steal the ball. There's no substitute for passing drills to get to know your teammates and develop your timing and accuracy in the open court.

When you bring the ball up, scan the entire court to see what opportunities are developing. Often you'll spot an open player and want to get him the ball in a split second without tipping off the defense. Don't get in the habit of looking only at the player to whom you'll pass. If the receiver is wide open it may be OK; if he's closely guarded, you may have to fake a pass in another direction first to draw his defender away, or choose an alternate receiver. Make sure the receiver sees you!

This is where peripheral vision—the ability to see out of the corners of your eyes as well as straight ahead—is helpful. Since you often need to pass without looking directly at your target, you need visual memory as well as muscle memory. Muscle memory tells you how much snap and force to put on the ball to hit your target. Visual memory means you can take a quick peek at your target, look elsewhere and still keep a picture of the target in your mind's eye. This takes concentration and focus; you cannot allow yourself to be distracted.

Coming upcourt, you should try to penetrate deeply enough that you can throw shorter passes which carry less risk of an interception. A common mistake is stopping the dribble too high when you're challenged by a defender. This is why you need a crossover dribble and need to be able to dribble well with both hands. If you do stop, protect the ball and call for help; don't try to force the ball into a crowd. A taller player has less trouble getting open and should come to you for the ball.

Passing is a matter of split-second timing. Once you've decided to pass, go ahead unless your intended receiver isn't looking at you or is suddenly covered by a defender. It's always good to have a second and third option in mind. Never force a pass just for the sake of getting rid of the ball.

Confidence is an essential ingredient in passing. Your teammates will sense your confidence and know you'll get the ball to them in the right place at the right time. Keep focused, keep the entire court in your vision, and snap off your passes quickly and accurately.

REVIEW

1. Think like a winner. Take pride in your passing so you can set up scoring opportunities for your teammates.
2. Practice all types of passes, beginning with the basics, and learn instinctively how to choose the right pass for any situation.
3. Control the ball with your fingertips.
4. Only pass when you have complete control of the ball.
5. Step, snap and follow through on your passes until these motions become second nature. Work on developing a quick release while maintaining accuracy.
6. Learn to adjust the force of your passes to the distance between you and the receiver. A bit too hard is better than too soft. Learn your effective passing range and try to stay within it.
7. Practice passing to spots. Work on hitting your target until it becomes second nature. Learn to "lead" teammates with passes by visualizing your target on bounce passes and lob passes.
8. Learn to pass both right and left. Don't begin every play by passing in the same direction. Vary your passes to keep the defense off balance.
9. Learn to pass without looking directly at your target. But also make sure the receiver sees you.
10. Keep focused, keep the entire court in your field of vision, keep the play in front of you. If you penetrate too far to see where your teammates are, and you do not have an open shot, pass to a teammate who's in a better position to see.
11. Avoid the fancy passes or the blind passes. Master the basics first.
12. Never force a bad pass just to get rid of the ball. Learning when not to pass is just as important as learning when not to dribble.

YOUR DAILY PRACTICE CHECKLIST:

Practice getting passes off quickly and accurately. Avoid always looking directly at your target.

___ Two hand chest passes to a stationary target—left, right, center

___ Two hand chest passes leading a moving target—left, right, center

___ Two hand chest passes off the dribble—left, right, center

___ Two hand bounce passes to a stationary target—left, right, center

___ Two hand bounce passes leading a moving target—left, right, center

___ Two hand bounce passes off the dribble to a stationary target—left, right, center

___ Two hand bounce passes off the dribble leading a moving target—left, right, center

___ Two hand overhead passes to a stationary target—left, right, center

___ Two hand lob passes leading a moving target—left, right, center

___ One hand bounce passes to a stationary target—left, right, center

___ One hand bounce passes leading a moving target—left, right, center

___ Hook passes to a teammate with each hand from a stationary position

___ Hook passes to a teammate with each hand while you're moving toward the basket

___ Overhand (baseball) passes, court-length and half-court length

If you think I want you to devote a lot of practice time to passing, go to the head of the class!

SHOOTING

I remember reading an article many years ago on a well-known college basketball coach. He was quoted as saying, "Shooting can't be taught. Either you have it or you don't."

I disagree. Yes, great shooters are gifted with a natural "touch." But if you don't have a natural touch, you can still develop effective shooting technique with practice. If a coach observes flaws in your technique, hopefully he or she will give you suggestions on how to improve.

Coaches, however, generally want to spend more practice time on strategy than fundamentals. So be prepared to develop good shooting technique on your own. Once you learn the basics—which is what this chapter is about—you can improve rapidly if you practice faithfully and intelligently.

I personally have seen a poor shooter transform himself into an excellent one: Wayne Embry, my teammate for many years on the Cincinnati Royals, later a key member of the Boston Celtics, and later still the general manager of the Milwaukee Bucks and then the Cleveland Cavaliers.

At 6'8" and 250 pounds, Wayne was known as "The Big Fella." Few opponents could match his strength when he played at Miami University of Ohio, so he took up residence under the basket and scored on layups, follow shots and short hooks. As the shortest center in the NBA, however, and facing players who were equally strong, he needed to add an outside shot to his repertoire.

Wayne worked harder at becoming a better shooter than anyone I've ever seen. He increased the range of his hook shot, and mastered shooting it with either hand. More important, he developed an effective jump shot from 10-15 feet. Now he could draw an opponent's center out of the key and clear the lanes to the basket so I could drive more often, which opened up our offense considerably.

DEVELOP A VARIETY OF SHOTS AND MOVES

If you play the pivot, you should be able to shoot facing the basket *and* with your back to it. As you transition from high school to college or college to the pros, you may have to change positions from center to forward or forward to guard. You'll need an outside shot and better moves to the basket.

Whatever position you play, you should be able to score from both inside and outside. Otherwise your game is too one-dimensional and you give the defense the advantage. Be able to shoot from a stationary position, off the dribble, coming off a screen, and most critically, moving to your left. That puts you way ahead of the game. Even most pros can't do it. I built my game around that capability.

Try to master as many shots as you can, along with the moves necessary to set them up. If you have the quickness to drive to the basket, you'll need several different inside shots and moves to help you score against taller defenders. If the defense knows you're always a threat to go to the basket, they will play you accordingly and that opens up your scoring opportunities from outside as well.

It's called basketball, but the game is about much more than one person putting the ball in the basket. It's also about dribbling, which is the basis for one-on-one play; passing and setting picks to help your teammates score; rebounding at both ends of the court; and moving intelligently without the ball to get into position for a shot. These principles are also addressed in the chapter on Offense.

Basic launch position: The ball should nest comfortably in your shooting hand, fingers spread wide enough to control the ball, wrist cocked. The more you cock your wrist, the higher an arch you'll get on the ball. Snap your wrist and release the ball off your fingertips; this release produces a natural spin. Only your fingers should touch the ball as you release it. Your "off" hand guides the ball as you bring it up to shoot. A good follow-through in the direction of the shot (right) ensures more accuracy.

A. THE BASIC PRINCIPLES OF SHOOTING

Shooting is primarily a matter of touch, rhythm and concentration. Touch means you apply just the right amount of force and spin to propel the ball the exact distance from your hand to the basket. Touch, Rhythm and Body Control are the physical aspects of shooting. The mental aspects, which are equally important, are Concentration, Confidence, Shot Selection and Making Adjustments.

1. DEVELOPING YOUR SHOOTING TOUCH

Most beginning players shoot too hard and too flat (with no arch on the ball). If you follow the steps I'm going to give you, you'll develop a better shooting touch. You can work on your touch any time, even when you're not on a basketball court! Your shooting touch comes from:

- Releasing the ball properly
- Developing an efficient shooting motion
- Putting the proper arch and spin on the ball

RELEASE THE BALL WITH YOUR WRIST AND FINGERTIPS

Cradle the ball in your hand with your fingers spread comfortably, but wide enough that you have control of the ball. Don't tense your fingers or try to squeeze the ball in a death grip; let the ball nest in your hand. Cock your wrist back so your hand is at an angle of anywhere from 45 to 90 degrees. The more you cock your wrist, the higher you'll want to raise your hand and elbow.

Snap your wrist and release the ball off your fingertips. This release puts a spin on the ball. Only your fingers should touch the ball as it leaves your hand. If the heel of your hand is touching the ball, either your wrist is too stiff or your fingers aren't spread enough to control the ball properly.

The wrist/fingertip release is the most critical part of shooting and passing. Practice it any time and anywhere you have a basketball handy. Flick your wrist and spin the ball off your fingertips, over and over. Practice with each hand, not just your dominant hand. Practice with two hands, over-handed and underhanded. This helps you develop "soft hands" and a better feel for the ball.

Feel comfortable with the ball. Think of it as a natural extension of your hand. If your hands aren't large enough to control the ball comfortably with the fingers of one hand, then use two. Your "off" hand can steady the ball until you release it with your shooting hand.

By mastering your release first, you can avoid two common mistakes: (1) shooting with a stiff wrist, and (2) shotputting the ball from shoulder or chest level. Beginners develop these habits because they don't have enough arm strength to shoot long shots any other way. Both habits are counter-productive to developing a good shooting touch. The trick is to master the release first and then shoot only from distances where you can use the proper release. That's one reason you must be able to dribble well, so you can get into position for close shots instead of only shooting from outside.

2. DEVELOP AN EFFICIENT SHOOTING MOTION

Strength is important in shooting, but accurate shooting is actually more a matter of efficient mechanics and good hand-eye coordination. You've seen skinny pitchers who can throw 95-mph fastballs for strikes, and much stronger pitchers who cannot, as the saying goes, "throw hard enough to raise a red spot." The same principle applies in basketball.

Hand-eye coordination means that in the blink of an eye, you measure the distance from your hand to the basket and visualize the path you want your shot to travel. Some players visualize the center of the basket as the target and aim over the rim; others visualize the back of the rim.

You don't aim by looking at the ball as you shoot; you focus on the basket and aim by "feeling" the ball as it leaves your hand. Your wrist and fingers put the necessary force and spin on the ball to send it along the path you've visualized. If you feel the shot properly in your fingers, you'll be able to sense whether or not it's on target as the ball leaves your hand.

A good shooting motion is smooth, continuous and energy-efficient, flowing from the legs, arms, wrist and fingers in that order. (1) Your legs elevate your body to the level at which you want to release the ball. (2) Your shooting arm is the catapult, raising the ball into position and following through after the shot is launched; your other arm helps guide and steady the ball. (3) Your wrist is the spring that launches the ball. The angle of your wrist determines the arch of the shot. (4) Your fingers cradle the ball and cause it to spin as it is released off the fingertips.

DEVELOP A QUICK, ACCURATE RELEASE

Where should you release the ball? The main considerations are (1) comfort, (2) efficiency of motion, (3) quickness of release, and (4) accuracy. Don't hesistate to experiment until you find the release point that works best for you. If you release the ball at eye level or overhead, the wrist snap and fingertip release will come more naturally to you.

FOLLOW-THROUGH

Follow-through is essential in shooting a basketball, just as in pitching a baseball or passing a foot-ball. Your arm should continue on line toward the target after you release the ball. It's unnatural to stop your motion abruptly once the ball has been released. Follow through with your arm on a true course and there's a better chance the ball will stay on a true course.

Release points: Shoulder level (left) You can release the ball at shoulder level, but be especially conscious of snapping your wrist so the ball spins off your fingertips. Many beginners try to "shotput" the ball from this position and shoot clunkers as a result. Bring the ball back over your shoulder for more spin. Generally, the higher the point of release, the better arch and spin you'll have on the ball.

Eye level (center) is probably your best point for a quick release. Many shooters prefer eye level or higher because they feel they can aim the ball better. This is an illusion, as you actually "feel" your aim in your arm, wrist and hand as your eyes focus on the basket. As you develop "muscle memory" for your shooting motion, you'll know as the ball leaves your hand whether or not it's on target.

Overhead (right): An overhead release is harder to block and produces good arch and spin. Here the shooter's forearm is straight up, which means the wrist supplies most of the power; if you bring the ball back over your head a bit, your upper arm can help with the launch. Experiment to find the release point and shooting motion that give you maximum accuracy and a smooth, quick release.

PUT AN ARCH ON YOUR SHOTS

A straight line is the shortest distance between two points, but it's probably not the path you want your shots to take. Straight shots can put you at a disadvantage because: (1) They're easier to block. (2) They tend to rebound more sharply, cutting down on your teammates' chances of a tip-in. (3) They're harder to adjust to the height of the basket. (4) They have less spin than shots with an arch. The more arch and spin on the ball, the better your chances of a basket even if the shot isn't dead center. You want more than your share of "lucky" shots? Put an arch and spin on the ball.

If you release the ball off your fingertips, putting an arch on the ball will start to come naturally. The angle of your wrist as you release the ball will determine the height of the arch. Larger angle (wrist cocked further back), higher arch; smaller angle (hand straight up), lower arch.

Putting an arch on your shot gives you several important advantages: (1) You have more control over the path of the shot. (2) You can adjust the shot better to variations in the height of the basket and the height and leaping ability of different defenders. (3) A missed shot takes a truer bounce and has a better chance of rebounding to a teammate. (4) If the shot hits the inside (or even the outside) of the rim, the ball could rotate into the basket anyway. (5) It's simply a more artistic shot. Put a "rainbow" on the ball and you could earn a pot of gold.

PRACTICE INTELLIGENTLY

Knowing how to practice shooting is as important as proper technique. Many players practice shooting exactly the wrong way. As soon as they take the court they start bombing away from 18–20 feet or more. Trying to force long shots immediately throws off your natural shooting motion.

Instead, start out under the basket with layups and short bank shots. Flick the ball into the basket over and over. Get a feel for the ball, the board and the basket. Concentrate on releasing the ball with your wrist and fingertips, producing enough spin and arch to clear the rim and drop cleanly into the center of the net, or to hit the board at the right angle to bank into the basket.

Don't worry about distance. You're training yourself to create a path to the basket by applying spin and arch to your shots as opposed to aiming straight at the basket. As "muscle memory" takes over and you have more command of your touch, gradually increase the distance. The important thing is not how many shots you shoot or from what distance, but the quality of each shot you take.

Meanwhile, to increase your shooting range, off the court you can work on improving your upper body strength with pushups, pullups and curls, and your wrist strength with hand grips and squeezing a rubber ball.

3. BODY CONTROL

While your arm, wrist and fingertips actually launch the ball, good shooting technique involves the entire body. You want to have good balance, and be "squared off" to the basket. That means your shoulders, and ideally your entire body, should be directly facing the basket. This gives you a better look at the basket, helps you aim better, and helps you get more force behind your shot. If you bank your layups off the board, ideally you want to be "square" to the board.

Whether you're shooting a jump shot, where your liftoff comes from both feet; on the move off your pivot foot (i.e. hook shot, layup); or from a stationary position, your shooting motion should have a smooth rhythm to it, with no wasted motion. The more efficient your shooting technique, the quicker and more accurately you'll be able to get your shots off.

In driving to the basket, body control also means that your torso is flexible enough to go over, under, around and between defenders. Sometimes your legs are facing in one direction and your upper body in another. In the chapter on conditioning, I talk about ways to develop this flexibility.

4. CONCENTRATION

Up to this point, we've covered the physical aspects of shooting. Now we address the mental aspects. Technique will take you only so far. You must master the mental aspects of shooting to realize your full potential. Concentration is foremost among them.

Concentration on the basket is an essential part of good shooting technique. Wherever you are on the court, you should have a mental image of where you are in relation to the basket, so that when you shoot, you're already locked in on your target. If you bank shots off the board, you need mental images of your target points. To create these images, you have to practice banking your shots off the board from different angles and distances.

When you need to get a shot off quickly, you don't always have time to set, square and shoot. Often you're aiming at the same time as you're going up for the shot. If you concentrate properly, your mind will call up the appropriate mental picture of your target, wherever you are on the court.

Some players shoot the eyes out of the basket in practice, but can't buy a basket in games. Their technique hasn't changed, so what has? They can't concentrate. They're distracted by crowd noise, or intimidated by physical contact. They can't adjust to a different background (people in the seats vs. empty seats), or they feel pressured with the clock running and hurry their shots. To shoot well in games, you have to block out distractions, keep your cool, and concentrate only on your target.

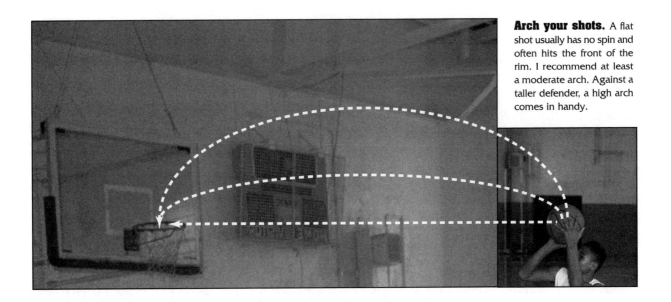

Arch your shots. A flat shot usually has no spin and often hits the front of the rim. I recommend at least a moderate arch. Against a taller defender, a high arch comes in handy.

Concentration requires both physical and mental toughness. When you shoot, the defender will often make physical contact with you, or threaten to. You can't play scared, and you can't shy away from contact. You must focus on the basket so intently that you're not distracted by the defender's tactics. Don't tense up; stay cool, stay in control, stay with your natural shooting rhythm.

5. Confidence

During a basketball game, you're confronted with hundreds of decisions. You have to be confident enough in your judgement to make each decision in a split second. Hesitation leads to missed opportunities, blocked shots and turnovers. If you make a wrong decision, or you make the right decision but a teammate messes up, you don't agonize over it, you move on to the next decision.

Confidence, like concentration, comes from mastering both the physical and mental aspects of the game. The physical aspect comes with practice (repetition), the mental aspect comes from your belief in yourself. Some players radiate confidence from the moment they step on the court; others never develop it. A team that plays with discipline and confidence can beat a more talented team.

Nothing improves your game or sharpens your confidence like competing against the best players available. Every game you play should be a learning experience. Make a mental note of what worked and what didn't, so you know what to work on in practice the next day.

Being confident doesn't mean you don't get nervous. Athletes naturally get nervous before big games, and some before every game, which is actually a good thing. That's how your body tunes up to meet the physical demands you're about to make on it. Once the game is under way, muscle memory and mental preparation should take over and the jitters usually vanish pretty quickly.

One of the biggest obstacles to developing confidence is worrying about what might go wrong. That takes all the fun out of the game. If you're afraid of missing a shot, you may hesitate to take the shot. You should *know* every shot is going in the minute it leaves your hand. Nobody is going to make every shot. But you have to believe you will.

If you miss a shot, don't get discouraged and pass up the same shot again in a similar situation. Keep taking good shots and eventually they'll fall. Coaches will rarely discourage you from taking good shots, even if you're not connecting. Coaches will, however, sit you down quickly for forcing a shot you have no business taking, or not passing to a teammate who's open for a better shot.

6. Shot Selection

Throughout this book, I stress the importance of taking good shots. What's a good shot? It's a shot (1) you know you'll make; (2) you're ready to take without hesitating; (3) your defender is unlikely to block; (4) the highest percentage shot available at that moment; and (5) the best shot for that particular situation. The rhythm of the game also affects shot selection. Sometimes you take certain shots for the psychological effect they have on your team, your opponent, or both.

If you have a lock on 15-foot jumpers from a certain spot and you're open for that shot, that's a good shot. It's an even better shot if you have teammates under the basket to rebound. If you're open for the 15-footer but a teammate is wide open under the basket, it's not a good shot. If your team needs a three-point shot, or one of your teammates has the "hot hand," or a teammate is guarded by a defender who's in foul trouble, then what would normally be a good shot for you may not be the best shot for that particular situation.

Another criterion for a good shot is that it feels natural. You don't have to force it. You've heard the expression "playing within yourself?" This means you're honest about your capabilities and have the discipline to stick with what you do best, unless circumstances demand otherwise. You know your effective shooting range, your best spots, how well you shoot when you're open as opposed to closely guarded, and your level of confidence in each shot.

That's shot selection in a perfect world. Then there are times when you have to play "beat the clock." So you devote a certain amount of individual practice time to those shots as well—blind shots, three-point shots, deep baseline shots, shots from the backcourt (I shot mine like a running hook shot for better touch and distance). You may never have to take one of those shots in a game, but it never hurts to be prepared. Luck tends to smile on those who are best prepared.

7. Making Adjustments

Along with talent and concentration, the ability to adjust is what sets the great shooters apart. Even if you have outstanding technique and you're totally focused, you still have to adjust to game and individual conditions, such as being sick, injured or fatigued. A good definition of a professional is someone who shows up and performs well even when he or she doesn't feel like it.

Adjustments are mental as well as physical. If you think like a winner, you'll instinctively know what adjustments you need to make individually and as a team. More than anything else, it's a matter of dealing with the reality of the present moment. You don't beat yourself up over what isn't working, or what should be working; you start with what *is* working and concentrate on doing what it takes to get back on track in order for your team to win.

In a game, if you're taking what ordinarily for you would be good shots but your shots aren't falling, you can't call "time out" and practice until your shot returns. You may need to adjust the arch, the release point, or the amount of force you put on your shots; I do not advise changing your basic shooting rhythm if it normally works for you. In your next practice, you can put in extra work on the shot that gave you trouble. Meanwhile, (1) Take a deep breath and make sure you're totally focused. Lack of concentration causes more misses than poor technique. (2) Take the same shot a step or two closer to the basket. (3) Shoot only layups or close-in shots until your touch returns. (4) Look for more opportunities to pass to teammates who have open shots.

When your outside shots aren't falling, one of the best remedies is to work for open shots under the basket, or drive to the hoop and draw fouls so you can shoot free throws. Many a player whose outside shot has gone bye-bye finds his touch returning after a drive to the basket for a layup, a

Practice intelligently. Start your shooting practice each day with close-in shots, over the rim or off the board. Work from both sides and with both hands. Get a feel for the ball, the board, the rim. Get a good rhythm going. After you've warmed up this way, then work at longer distances. Mix in some free throws with your layups and bank shots—that duplicates a situation you'll often face in a game. Regardless of how high you jump, and whether you aim directly at the basket or use the board, be sure to concentrate on your target, square your body to the basket, release the ball properly and follow through, as the shooter in the left photo demonstrates.

Making adjustments. If you get in the habit of practicing intelligently, you'll find it easier to adjust in games. When your outside shot isn't connecting, work your way in closer to the basket and take shorter shots. If you draw double coverage, get the ball to an open teammate for a score. Making a couple of baskets in close will help you regain your confidence and your outside shot will come back.

close-in bank shot, a tip-in or a free throw. It's just like bunting to break a batting slump in baseball. The close-in shot breaks the spell and helps you regain confidence in your outside shot. All athletes go through dry spells. That's when you have to get tougher and more determined. You may need to relax a bit more; you can relax and still stay focused. Maybe you're pressing too hard, or rushing your shots without being aware of it.

If you're getting shots blocked, you may need to take different shots, or have your teammates set screens for you. If your opponents play an extremely physical game, do not allow yourself to be intimidated; take advantage of their aggressiveness and draw them into fouls. Once you have an idea as to what you need to do in order to adjust, talk it over with your coach and teammates to make sure everyone knows what's happening.

B. YOUR REPERTOIRE OF SHOTS

One of the best things you can do for yourself is to master as many types of shots as possible—not just the shooting motion, but the ability to shoot from different spots on the court, with either hand, while moving left or right, and off of various moves. You also have to know which shots you can always depend on, which ones are still a bit shaky and need more practice, and which ones simply do not work for you. You have to know your effective shooting range for each shot.

Every player has to be able to shoot layups. If you shoot nothing but layups, and can make free throws when you're fouled while shooting layups, you'll get your share of points.

I feel every player, regardless of position, ought to be able to shoot a hook shot. It's easy to learn and gives you an added weapon in situations close to the basket. Then ideally, every player should have an outside shot of some kind, from at least a 12–18 foot range. Most players prefer jump shots, but there's nothing wrong with a one-hand push shot or even a two-hand set if you can get the shot off quickly and accurately and it works better for you than a jump shot.

1. THE LAYUP

My favorite shot has always been the layup. Sure, the longer shots are more spectacular, but the layup is the highest-percentage shot. My game was based on going to the hoop whenever there was even the slightest opening. Plus which, I always felt that if I could penetrate close enough to the basket for a layup, I had better than a 50-50 chance of drawing a foul and making it a three-point play. Once I drove for the basket, I was going to make the layup whether I got fouled or not.

You should make 100% of your layups. The only reason not to make a layup should be that you were so severely fouled that your shooting motion was interrupted.

Your first and only priority in shooting a layup is to put the ball in the basket, not to impress the crowd or show up the defensive player. The simpler you keep the shot, the better your chance of making it. I recommend banking the ball off the board whenever possible instead of laying the ball up over the front of the rim.

Whether you're driving for the basket off your dribble or leading a fast break, you have to be aware of (1) your angle to the basket, (2) your speed, (3) how closely you're guarded, (4) the defender's angle to you, quickness, height, and leaping ability. You may be coming in from the baseline, from a 45-degree angle on the court, or straight toward the basket. You may be guarded by your own defender, you may be picked up by another defender, or you may be wide open.

If you're driving the lane and you're guarded, you'll generally want to shoot with the hand away from the basket so your body is between the defender and the ball. From the right side of the basket, your right hand; left side, left hand. Otherwise the shot's too easy to block. That's why you need to be able to shoot layups with either hand. Too many players, even in the pros, can only shoot with one hand. So if the defense forces them to the other side of the basket, they're out of luck, unless they can maneuver around underneath the basket for a reverse layup.

If you're driving the baseline or from an angle on the court, and you've beaten your defender, use whichever hand and method of release (overhand or underhand) give you better control of the shot. (You may start your drive with one shot in mind and have to adjust if you're challenged by another defender.) Keep your head up and concentrate 100% on the goal. If you're going to use the board, visualize your target and lay the ball up against the target so it bounces naturally into the basket from that angle.

A soft touch is critical in shooting layups. You control the ball with your wrist and fingers just as if you were shooting outside shots. If you don't use the board, flip the ball over the rim with a slight arch instead of just clearing the rim. If you use the board, just lay the ball up against the right spot on the board and don't worry as much about the spin. Having the correct angle to the board is more important in a layup than the amount of spin you put on the ball. You should spend some practice time learning how the ball bounces off the board, and how live or dead the rim is.

The layup is the most basic shot in basketball, and most players don't practice it nearly enough. You must be able to shoot layups from either side and with either hand. Learn the spots on the board that give you the truest bounce into the basket. Practice coming in from different angles, always concentrating 100% on your target (usually the square above the basket). Forget the razzle-dazzle moves and focus on executing the shot properly. Extend yourself fully as you go up. If you "coast," hold back or tense up, you can blow the shot.

Practice layups every day and get your layups down cold before you start shooting from outside. Work on driving to the basket from different angles. Practice layups with either hand, just as you practice dribbling with either hand. (Dribbling and layups work together!) If you really want to improve your game, devote additional practice time to shooting layups and dribbling with your weaker hand. Make sure you shoot off the correct foot. Shooting a layup righthanded, your left foot will be the pivot foot or launch foot; shooting lefthanded, it will be the right foot.

I've seen players at all levels take layups for granted, and miss the shot at a critical point in a game. You can never take layups for granted; you need 100% concentration. Some players "hear footsteps" and tense up in fear of getting hit by a defender, which throws off their natural shooting motion. Or they get distracted by the background or the crowd noise. But the biggest mistake players make in shooting layups, particularly off a fast break, is coasting at the end of the drive. Extend yourself fully and follow through! Otherwise you develop sloppy shooting habits.

I prefer an overhand shooting motion for layups, because you're fully extended and the shot is harder to block. Sometimes you may shoot underhanded in an attempt to draw a foul, or simply because you feel more comfortable shooting that way. If you're driving toward the basket against taller players, a "running hook shot" off a slight fadeaway move can be an excellent weapon. You should develop a variety of shots so you can adjust to the way you're guarded at any given time.

Once you have absolutely mastered the basic layups, then you can work on reverse layups, spin-around shots, finger rolls and other moves you keep in reserve for situations when you're tightly guarded and have no other way of getting off a shot or a pass.

If you shoot your layup over the rim instead of banking it off the board, be sure to extend fully and loft the ball over the rim with a gentle touch. Work on this shot with each hand! Shooting layups lefthanded (photo at right) may not feel natural at first if you're righthanded, which is all the more reason to work on the shot. Make sure your right foot is your pivot/launch foot when you shoot the shot lefthanded. Being able to dribble and shoot well with either hand puts you far ahead of the competition.

DUNKING

What do I think about dunking? I think it's way overrated. You get no extra points for a dunk. I took pride in being able to drive to the hoop and shoot a variety of shots with accuracy and finesse, drawing fouls in the process a good deal of the time. I know this makes me old-fashioned, but that's the way I feel.

The worst aspect of basketball today is the overemphasis on the dunk and the three-point shot at the expense of good fundamentals. Both are crowd-pleasers, but good solid outside shooting has taken a beating as a result. There's so much uninformed talk about the "vertical game" and "playing above the rim." The game is played on a horizontal court 94 feet by 50 feet. You might actually see dunks in a game 6–10 times. Most rebounds are taken at a level below the rim, did you know that? My advice is that you not worry so much about developing your "vertical leap" and instead focus on becoming a fundamentally sound, all-around basketball player.

2. THE JUMP SHOT

You may find this hard to imagine, but when I began my pro career, many players still shot with one or both feet on the floor: hook shots, one-hand push shots, two-hand set shots and overhead shots. The jump shot revolutionized basketball. Back then, you might have one or two good jump-shooters on a team; now, everyone is expected to shoot the jumper. Some of the "old-fashioned" shots, by the way, could be just as effective today as three-point shots as jump shots are, but no one wants to shoot them any more.

82

During my pro career, practically every team ran the fast break as often as possible. The Boston Celtics dominated the league and you had to run to keep pace with them. There were also many more outstanding rebounders who could clear the ball out quickly to start a fast break. The jump shot lent itself to this up-tempo game. Jump shooters could trail the fast break, or if they were dribbling, pull up and shoot from outside if the lane was clogged.

Today, there's more emphasis on three-point shots, the half-court game, and, supposedly, on defensive tactics that take away the fast break. Personally, I think "stronger defense" is just an excuse for much of the poor shooting I see today.

The main advantage of the jump shot is the element of surprise. You know when you'll shoot, your defender does not. The jump gives you a split-second advantage before the defender can react, and an efficient shooting motion can also help you put more force behind the ball.

As with any other shot, your jump shot must be a smooth, continuous motion: legs, arms, wrist and fingertips. If your jump and your shot feel like two separate motions, you're not shooting efficiently.

Some players worry too much about vertical leap when quickness, good court position, rhythm and concentration are all much more important. Larry Bird couldn't jump worth a darn, and his jump shot was really more of a one-hand push shot, but he sure got open for a lot of those shots and made them. (He grabbed a lot of rebounds, too.)

However high you jump, you want to release the ball at the peak of your leap. Some players leap first, then bring the ball up to shoot. This technique is less efficient and slows down your release. You should bring the ball into position to shoot as you leap. The squareoff, leap, setup and shot should all be one continuous motion.

Your shooting style is an individual matter, like a baseball pitching delivery or batting stance; above all, it should feel natural and comfortable. Some players bring the ball up with the shooting hand; most guide it with the off hand. The release point could be shoulder level, eye level, or overhead. Some players jump straight up, some jump into the defender (thinking it's a slick way to beg for fouls), some jump backward (a fadeaway motion).

Jump shots: Concentration, good shooting rhythm and a good wrist/fingertip release that puts arch and spin on the ball are all more important than vertical leap. Release the ball wherever it feels most natural and follow through.

My own shooting style was developed on Indianapolis playgrounds as a reaction to having my shots blocked by taller players when I was 12 years old and 5'6" tall. I figured out that (1) If I dribbled lefthanded, I was dribbling away from the defender with the hand farthest from the defender. (2) If I jumped slightly backward as I shot, I was even farther from the defender. I could square off to the basket facing the defender or angled to him. (3) If I released the ball above my head with my wrist cocked back, I got a natural wrist/fingertip release *and* a higher arch over the defender's hand.

Even though I was jumping away from the basket, the overhead release actually gave me more power from my upper arm muscles and the hinge action of my elbow; most shooters use only their wrist and forearm. The main thing I had to master was the exchange, bringing the ball up off the dribble with my left hand and transferring it to my shooting hand while I was jumping. I do not recommend a turnaround or fallaway jumper, by the way, unless it feels completely natural to you.

As long as you protect the ball, concentrate on the basket and aim accurately, your jump and release point do not matter nearly as much as a good wrist/fingertip release, arch and spin. Get the shot off smoothly and quickly. If you're too slow to set up, your shot is more likely to be blocked.

When you receive a pass and you're in position to shoot, should you shoot immediately or dribble first? You have to know the defense. I'd dribble once, twice at most or go on to another move. When should you shoot coming off a screen? I wouldn't use a screen if you know the defender is anticipating it, or you've already used a screen two or three times in a row. If a taller player is being screened, go a step or two beyond the screen; otherwise he may take a step out and block your shot.

To avoid getting your shots blocked, vary your pattern of shooting, not your shooting technique. (Getting a shot blocked is not fatal, by the way; you have a 50-50 chance of getting the ball back.) You want to avoid becoming predictable. Defenders remember if you always dribble a certain number of times before you shoot, always shoot moving in the same direction, always shoot from directly behind a screen instead of taking a step beyond, always shoot from the same spots.

Shooting on the move: If you can shoot while moving toward the basket, the defender doesn't know whether to play you for a jump shot or a layup. If you can catch the defender flatfooted for a split second, you can get your shot off even against a taller player. You should also be able to pass off this same move. Suggestions: When the defender is in bodily contact with you (left photo), be sure you're not suckered into a charging foul. Using your left hand for a layup off the board instead of driving straight for the basket would be a higher-percentage shot. If you've already beaten the defender (right photo), I would go on to the basket and shoot a layup. If you hesitate for a moment en route, often you can get the defender to run into you as you're shooting and wind up with a three-point play.

You should be able to shoot jump shots from a standing position and on the move, i.e., around the perimeter, coming off a screen, trailing the fast break, moving toward the basket. You can use fakes to give yourself shooting space when you're closely guarded. Examples: fake a pass and then shoot; fake with your head or the ball to get the defender to leave his feet; start your dribble as if you were going to drive for the basket, then pull up and shoot.

In practicing your jump shot, strive for accuracy within a certain range instead of always shooting from the same spots. It's natural to feel more confident when you're locked in on the target from a certain spot, i.e., 15 feet from the free throw line, 21 feet from the top of the key. But if you restrict yourself to certain spots, defenders will get there first and deny your shots. Develop a comfortable shooting radius, a distance from which you can always hit regardless of your angle to the basket. Practice in a circle: baseline, corner, 45-degree angle, free throw line, top of the key, then back around the other way.

When shooting from the side, should you bank your shot off the board or aim straight at the basket? I recommend using the board within 10–15 feet of the basket if your defender is in line between you and the basket. This applies to virtually any type of shot, not just jump shots.

STATIONARY SHOTS

Often a stationary shot will work where a jump shot will not, if for no other reason than the element of surprise. Instead of always shooting on the move, if you set up in one spot the defender may not be able to react quickly enough to catch up with you.

3. THE HOOK SHOT

It's not competely accurate to call the hook shot a stationary shot, because you often shoot it while you're on the move.

Contrary to popular opinion, the hook shot is not the exclusive property of centers only. It can be an effective offensive weapon for any player, especially one who's constantly overmatched height-wise. Shot properly, it's difficult to block.

The hook shot: Whatever position you play, you should develop a good hook shot, preferably with either hand. It's a valuable offensive weapon. You can hook over taller defenders as you move toward or away from the basket, off the same moves as if you were driving for a layup. Don't shoot flatfooted; bring up your knee on the same side as your shooting hand for a fluid motion and more power and accuracy. Remember the wrist/fingertip release. Spin the ball off your fingertips and arch the shot instead of shooting it on a straight line. Practice banking the hook shot off the board from either side as well as aiming it directly at the basket. The shooter here has turned a bit too much and is facing the basket more than I'd like; to protect the ball, it's better to have your body angled more between the ball and the defender as you release the shot.

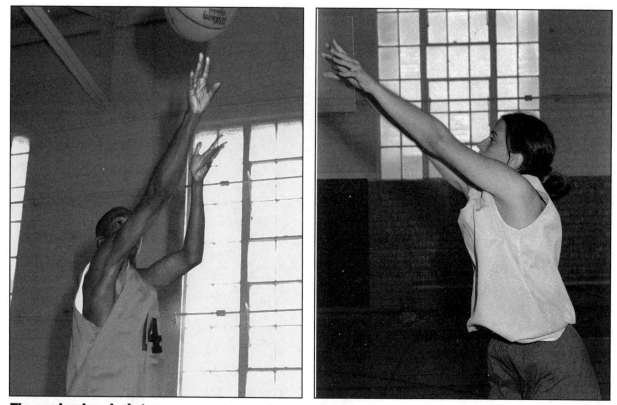

The one-hand push shot: Most players today use a one-hand push shot for free throws, but feel they have to shoot jump shots while the ball is in play. Sometimes you can shoot this shot more accurately than a jumper, which is why I feel it's a good shot to have in your repertoire. A slight bend at the knees gives you more power. Otherwise, it's concentration, wrist/fingertip release, arch and spin.

The two-hand set shot: Hardly anyone shoots this shot any more, yet it can be very effective. If you can throw an accurate lob pass, you can shoot a two-hand set; you're simply aiming at the basket instead of leading a receiver. You need a good wrist snap, fingertip release and follow-through for this shot. You can release the ball from chest, shoulder or eye level; a bit of a bend at the knees adds power.

A center will usually shoot the hook shot from a low post, somewhere in or alongside the lane. Guards and forwards should learn to shoot it on the move toward or away from the basket. This shot can be very effective against taller players when you're driving to the hoop. I could shoot the hook off a drive straight at the basket; or, starting up high, I'd execute a reverse pivot and back the defender toward the basket as I was dribbling. Once I was close enough, I wouldn't hesitate to use the hook if that was the best option.

If you're a center, you should have at least a 5–10 foot hook shot, ideally with either hand. The defense will try to force you in one direction or the other, so why not be able to shoot moving in either direction? Without a hook shot, you're wasting whatever height advantage you might have. You should shoot 100 hook shots a day with each hand! Whether you release the ball at shoulder height or over your head, and bank it off the board or aim directly for the basket, the shot should feel natural and comfortable. The hook shot is actually a more natural arm motion than any other shot, so you have a considerable advantage in developing the muscle memory for the shot.

The best hook shot I ever saw belonged to my Milwaukee Bucks teammate Kareem Abdul-Jabbar. Ironically, Kareem developed his "skyhook" after dunking was outlawed during his college days at UCLA. Once he had the rhythm down, he could shoot it from increasingly longer distances. Magic Johnson's "junior skyhook" was pretty effective as well.

Just as guards should learn to shoot hook shots, taller players should learn to shoot from outside. Variety is the key to scoring. If you have only one shot, someone will figure out a way to stop it. Whatever position you play, you should have at least one inside shot and one outside shot you can always rely on, and be able to get open for either. Then you can keep the defense off-balance.

4. THE ONE-HAND PUSH SHOT

You can shoot the one-hand push shot in as many different ways as you shoot a jump shot. The only difference is your feet don't leave the floor, although you may raise up on tiptoe. Don't shotput the ball; use the wrist/fingertip release from a comfortable release point—chest level, shoulder level, eye level, overhead—and follow through properly. A slight bend at the knees gives you more power.

5. THE TWO-HAND SET SHOT

Two-hand set shooting seems to be a lost art, but this shot can be effective if you can get it off quickly. It's just like a lob pass except you aim at the basket instead of leading a receiver. Wrist/fingertip release and follow-through are essential. If the wrist snap and follow-through feel natural, you're within your range; if you have to strain, and shoot with your arms instead of your wrists, you're outside your range. Bend your knees slightly and fire away from chest, shoulder or eye level.

REVIEW:

We've covered the principles of shooting and the mechanics of each shot in the repertoire. Now it's up to you to work hard, practice intelligently, and develop muscle memory and confidence!

1. Work on your wrist/fingertip release and follow-through so you can put arch and spin on the ball and develop a sure shooting touch.
2. Develop a smooth, efficient shooting rhythm. Experiment with various release points to find the one that enables you to get your shots off quickly and accurately.
3. Practice intelligently, beginning close to the basket. Work on your release and shooting rhythm first, then increase the distance as you warm up.
4. The mental aspects of shooting are just as important as the physical. Concentration is as important as proper release and efficient shooting rhythm.
5. When shooting layups, keep it simple, extend yourself fully and concentrate on the basket. The "easier" the shot, the more you need to concentrate.
6. Shoot layups with either hand so you can shoot with the hand farthest from the defender.
7. Proper release, efficient shooting rhythm and concentration are all more important than vertical leap in shooting jump shots. Get open for shots instead of trying to outjump defenders.
8. Know your effective range with various shots so you can make an intelligent shot selection.
9. Never hesitate to take a good shot unless a teammate is in even better scoring position.
10. Learn what adjustments you need to make if your outside shots aren't falling.
11. Whatever position you play, develop a hook shot. Centers should shoot it with either hand.
12. Play against the best competition possible to learn what you need to do to improve.

YOUR DAILY PRACTICE CHECKLIST:

___ Work on your wrist/fingertip release daily, whenever and wherever there's a ball handy.

___ Begin practice close to the basket with 100 bank shots and layups, 50 from each side.

___ Shoot free throws and outside shots after warming up properly close to the basket.

___ Know your effective shooting range and shoot from that radius in a circle around the court.

___ Shoot at least 100 layups with each hand while driving for the basket.

___ Shoot at least 100 jump shots from different spots, moving right, moving left, directly facing basket.

___ Shoot at least 50 hook shots with each hand, some from a post position, some off the dribble.

FREE THROW SHOOTING

Free throw shooting rates a special section by itself. In fact, entire books have been written on the subject. If you plan to play in any kind of organized competition, you had better become a master free throw shooter, for your own benefit and your team's. You certainly don't want to be the player the other team fouls any time they need the ball because they know you cannot make free throws.

A good free throw shooting team should win most of its games. A superior team that can't make free throws will lose games it should win. Fans boo a player who misses a crucial free throw late in a game, but missed free throws in the early minutes of the game are just as harmful.

Even if you never take part in organized competition, practice shooting free throws. It's a helpful exercise. If you're having trouble hitting your outside shots, shoot close-in shots and free throws. Concentrate on the basket and nothing else. Make sure you stay within your natural shooting rhythm and release the ball with your wrist and fingertips, applying the proper arch and spin just as you would to any other type of shot. You'll find your outside shooting touch coming back.

If you have pride in the way you play the game, never accept missing a free throw. Yes, you might miss occasionally, but here's an area where you can aim for perfection and know it's a realistic goal. You must promise never to let yourself get careless at the free throw line, in practice or games.

If your offensive game is based on going to the basket, as mine was, then you'd better shoot a lot of free throws in practice. One of the reasons you go to the basket is to draw fouls and create three-point scoring opportunities. Over my NBA career, I made almost as many free throws as I did field goals, never shooting less than 80% at the line, leading the league four times in total free throws and twice in free throw percentage. With the exception of one off year, I seemed to get more consistent at the line the longer I played.

RELAXATION AND CONCENTRATION ARE VITAL

How you shoot a free throw is not as important as your concentration on nothing but the basket. Free throw shooting is almost completely mental. Many players who are otherwise outstanding shooters get psyched when they shoot free throws. Their anxiety affects their concentration and mechanics. You already have the "muscle memory" to shoot the shot. Just relax and concentrate.

Since it is a *free* throw, you're free to use any style of shooting you wish, as long as you do not cross the foul line while shooting. If your best shot is a jump shot, use it. There have been several NBA players who shot jump shots for free throws.

Some coaches still prefer the two-hand underhand style of free throw shooting, but this is rarely in favor any more. One of the advantages of this style is that it almost forces you to release the ball off your fingertips, which naturally puts backspin on the ball. Almost everyone today shoots a one-hand push shot for a free throw, although some players use a two-hand set shot.

The main consideration in choosing your style is that you be completely relaxed, and shoot with a natural rhythm. You shouldn't even be conscious of your shooting mechanics, they should be so natural to you by this point. Breathe, aim, concentrate, release the shot and follow through.

Free throw shooting is mostly mental. Through practice, you should have already developed an efficient shooting rhythm and the necessary "muscle memory" to shoot free throws accurately. Now concentration has to take over. Breathe, relax, focus, aim, release the ball properly and follow through. For whatever reason, many players don't follow through as well on free throws as on other shots. Block out all distractions, all negative thoughts, and concentrate on the basket. Shoot at least 100 free throws a day. If you want to duplicate a game situation, run several wind sprints up and down the court and then shoot free throws. Or shoot free throws mixed in with shots driving to the basket.

The most universal style is one with the feet spread to shoulder width or a bit less, knees slightly bent, and the release point at eye level. My own style was a bit more exaggerated; I used basically the same catapult release as I did with my jump shot, "pulling the trigger" from overhead. I'm not advising you to copy it, but it was the style most comfortable for me. Also, I thought it made sense to use the same release for free throws as I did for jump shots when the ball was in play.

Once you've settled on a comfortable shooting style at the line, develop a good shooting rhythm. The big difference here is that you're under no pressure to get the shot off quickly, so your rhythm changes somewhat. The trick is not to let the change in rhythm lead to a falloff in concentration.

When you get right down to it, free throw shooting is a matter of mental toughness. You have to have the same focus and winning attitude at the line as you have in the rest of your game.

I urge you to shoot a hundred or more free throws in practice every day. That will make the mechanics second nature. To develop the mental toughness, you might find it helpful to shoot free throws after running wind sprints or mixed in with driving shots to the basket. This exercise will help you duplicate situations you'll face in games.

BASICS OF OFFENSE

The purpose of this book is to give you a program for improving your skills in the fundamentals of basketball. We don't get into specific offensive and defensive strategies, because those really are up to your coach. In this section, however, we do talk about certain basics of offensive play which any complete basketball player needs to learn in order to function well within any system.

Once you've gained some expertise in the fundamentals, and committed to constantly improving your skills in those areas, the mental aspect of basketball becomes as important as the physical. Basketball, after all, is a *game*, which means there is gamesmanship involved. Yes, you can compete on pure athletic skill, but you can compete even better when you know your opponents' strengths and weaknesses, know what's likely to work against them and what isn't, and can anticipate their moves in various situations. You also learn how to push a team's emotional buttons. You learn who quits when the going gets rough, who responds to the challenge, who gets rattled by mistakes or intimidated by physical contact, who lets anger negatively affect his or her performance.

One of the advantages of playing professionally is that you face the same players often enough to get to know them pretty well. You don't have this advantage in high school and college, where you might play a team at most two or three times a year. On the playground or at your local Boys and Girls Club, however, you often see the same players every day. Be observant on the court and learn to become a "quick study" of other players. This skill will serve you well in organized competition.

What did I learn over 14 years in the NBA? I learned immediately how important strength is, and built up the strength I needed to play my type of game. Otherwise, what I learned had to do more with the mental aspects of the game. I got to know the players better, got a better handle on when to take shots, when to pass, how to draw fouls, how to rally a team, how to crank up the tempo, how to keep momentum going. I had always felt that good precise play execution was preferable to razzle-dazzle anytime, and found this as true in the pros as at any other level of competition. I also developed more of an appreciation for role players, those who were not always the most gifted athletically, but knew and were willing to do what was required of them to help their teams win.

PLAYING YOUR ROLE

Not everyone can be a star, but everyone *can* contribute to his or her team's success. Unfortunately, many players are unable to accept a supporting role. They pout if they don't play a certain number of minutes or get a certain number of shots. The objective is to do whatever it takes to help your *team* win: set picks, clear the outlet pass after a rebound, take charging fouls.

On offense, most plays are not successful, so the game comes down to 1-on-1 or 2-on-2. What about the other three or four players? Should they stand and watch the players who have the ball? On a well-coached team, or a playground team with intelligent players, there's a role for everyone. If you're on the "weak side," i.e., the side of the court with fewer players, there are various ways to contribute. You can move to draw a defender away from the basket, or clear out the lane; come up to set a pick, or come to the ball when a teammate is double-teamed; block out under the basket, crash the board for an offensive rebound, or drop back quickly on defense in order to prevent a cheap basket. Always be alert for ways you can contribute and take pride in doing your job well.

The reverse pivot is a basic offensive move every player needs to learn. With your back to the basket, you plant one foot as your pivot foot, fake a half pivot in that direction and then pivot fully the other way. As you pivot back, get a good first step and dribble with the hand furthest from the defender. (Faking left and pivoting right, you'd dribble with your left hand.) Keep sliding your front foot far ahead as you move toward the basket so you can maintain inside position on the defender. Or you can reverse pivot, start toward the basket, then pull up and pass or shoot. As long as you continue your dribble, you can use either foot as your pivot foot when you stop.

If the weak side players on your team have no specific assignments, ask the coach what he or she wants you to do in those situations. If you have no assignment, ask if it's OK for you to freelance. Size up the game situation and figure out how you can best help your team. Look for opportunities such as I mentioned in the previous paragraph. In particular, a team can almost always use rebounding help on the weak side; if you're a forward, that should be your number one priority.

MOVING WITHOUT THE BALL

Being able to move without the ball is an essential part of playing offense. You have to move to get open for your own shots, and to set up shots for your teammates. Too often the good shooters have a tendency to stand in one spot and expect the ball to come to them. Once the defense sees that you aren't moving, they'll try to deny you the ball at the spots where you expect it.

There's a big advantage to moving without the ball. Defensive players are often conditioned to play the ball, and don't guard a player without the ball as closely. If you move without the ball, you'll often find yourself in the clear for a wide-open shot. Or you'll draw defensive coverage which opens up a teammate. If you do break open, don't hesitate to call for the ball. You've earned the good shot, now you can help your team by making it.

When you keep moving, you keep constant pressure on the defense, and have a better chance of wearing them down. If one player stands still, the overall flow of the offense slows down, and there are fewer options for the other players. Constant movement keeps the court opened up, the lanes clear, and there are more opportunities for you or a teammate to get open for a good shot.

Sometimes you move away from the ball at first, then back to it. At other times, you move to the ball immediately—for example, to exchange court position with a teammate, or to take the ball from a teammate who's double-teamed or otherwise tied up. In that situation, as soon as you have the ball your teammate should clear out of the area, or, depending on your position on the court, possibly work a pick-and-roll with you. If you play forward, and your team's guards are having trouble penetrating, you should come out to meet the ball (but not too high on the court).

It's only pick and roll, but I like it: The key to a successful pick and roll (players in the white shirts) is for the player with the ball to go a couple of steps past the pick (first photo, next page). This creates a vacuum so the player who set the pick can "roll" (turn to the basket). Otherwise the defender on the left can switch back to cut him off. The player who picks has to make sure the defenders switch before he rolls. The defender on the right probably could have fought through the pick instead of switching, but hesitated. Once the switch was made, he could have stepped back to cut off the "roll" to the basket.

Some of the basic routes you might run without the ball, depending on your position:
- Perimeter (i.e., around the 3-point line) or half perimeter (from the corner to the top of the key)
- Guards cross at the top of key
- Forward and guards cross on the wing (the side of the court)
- Forward rotates with the center
- Center clears out of the lane to the corner or baseline (especially if your defender sags)
- Forwards cross along the baseline
- Guard runs a circle pattern (baseline, under the basket, back to top of key)
- Guard or forward cuts to the basket from the top of the key, then out to the wing

Some important rules for moving without the ball (these are just common sense):
- Always keep your eye on the ball.
- Don't turn your back on your defender (he may double-team the player with the ball, or get position for an uncontested rebound).
- Don't overload one side of the court (except possibly against a zone defense).
- Move to the ball. Don't make your team force a bad pass, especially if you're double-teamed.
- Always keep moving. If you run a route and nothing happens, begin a new route.
- If you're a forward or center away from the flow of play, go for the offensive rebound.
- Most important: always keep your man blocked off the board.

SETTING SCREENS AND PICKS

Setting screens or picks for your teammates is another basic element of offensive play. In fact, one of the reasons you move without the ball is to get to a certain place on the court and set up a screen. A true team player contributes to the scoring by setting screens so other players can shoot. Coaches often design an offense to set up screens for the best shooters at certain points on the court. If no such plays are designed for you, don't pout; you'll get your points other ways: offensive rebounds, grabbing loose balls, driving for the hoop and getting fouled.

To set a pick properly, first make sure you *can* pick. You must stand directly in the path of a defender for a full second before moving. If you have to move to remain in that player's path, you can be called for an offensive foul. Get as much of your body as possible in front of the defender, otherwise he could slide past you and defeat the purpose of the pick. You can't shy away from a little body contact. Hold your position until you see what the defense does. In a well-executed pick, one

or more of these things should happen: the defender runs into you and draws a foul; the defender you picked has to switch with the defender guarding you; or your teammate gets open for a shot.

If you have the ball facing away from the basket, you can motion a teammate to come your way. As he cuts close to you, you pick off his defender, pass or hand him the ball, and he has an open shot. For centers and forwards, this is a basic part of your game. If you have the ball and want to set a screen for a shooter, be sure you protect the ball. Often the player with the ball pays too much attention to the movement of the other players and not enough attention to protecting the ball.

I've always felt a player should get an assist for setting a screen that leads directly to a basket, just as an assist is credited for a pass that leads directly to a basket.

THE PICK AND ROLL

The "pick and roll" is a basic offensive play. The purpose is to create a switch where a short defender winds up guarding a tall player who can take him inside and shoot over him, and a tall defender guards a shorter and quicker player who can drive around or shoot over him from outside. The taller offensive player (center or forward) picks for the shorter (usually a guard) who has the ball, then "rolls" (turns to the basket) when the ball-handler's defender makes contact with him. As the two defenders switch, creating the mismatch, the ball-handler should have an open pass to the player who's "rolling." The ball-handler can (1) dribble past the pick as his defender is picked and pass to the pick as he rolls to the basket, or (2) pass to the pick, run his defender into the pick, get the ball back and pass to the pick as he rolls to the basket. This second version is also called the "give and go."

The keys to a successful pick and roll are, for the player who picks and rolls:
- Make sure you *can* pick.
- Don't roll too fast; make sure (1) the defenders switch, (2) your teammate can get you the ball.
- Keep your eye on the ball as you're cutting for the basket.
- Avoid committing an offensive foul if another defender comes up to stop you as you roll.

For the player with the ball:
- Don't stop immediately behind the pick; move 1–2 steps beyond to create more of an opening for the player who set the pick and is now rolling toward the basket.
- Make sure the teammate rolling to the basket is open for a clear pass and sees you.
- Pass away from the defender, using the best pass for the situation (bounce, overhead, lob).

If you're the player with the ball, keep your eyes open for other possibilities. Don't force a pass to the player turning to the basket when someone else might be in even better position for a shot. Sometimes another defender comes up to stop the roll and leaves his man open to cut to the hoop.

RUNNING THE FAST BREAK

I've seen lots of players who could play half-court basketball all day long, but were lost whenever they had to play a full-court game. Playing full-court ball, especially a running game, requires a lot more speed, endurance, concentration and ball-handling skill than the half-court game does.

A fast break usually begins with an outlet pass after a defensive rebound (although some teams will try to fast break off the inbounds pass). Ideally, there are three players on the break, one in the middle with the ball and two in the "lanes" to either side of him, and one or two defenders back trying to stop them. The faster of the two players in the lanes cuts to the basket for a pass, and the other follows a step behind, ready to take a pass in a 2-on-1 situation, or follow up on the offensive board. A fourth player should "trail" in case the defense cuts off the lanes to the basket. The trailer is usually a good outside shooter who can pull up and hit from medium range; sometimes a fast and agile tall player trails the break, cuts to the basket unguarded and takes a lob pass for the score.

Sometimes it takes two, three or four passes to get the ball to an open player under the basket. Or the player in the middle (on the "point") dribbles upcourt far enough to hit the lead player with a single pass. Teams who run the fast break will run passing drills daily in practice to teach their players the various options available to them, get them used to handling the ball while moving at top speed, and give them an opportunity to develop timing as they learn each other's capabilities.

In playground basketball, a fast break is often more like a train wreck, because the players don't know each other's skills well enough or they try to get too fancy with their passes and moves to the basket. Forcing passes on the fast break almost always results in turnovers. If one of the lead players on the break can't get open for a pass within the ball-handler's effective passing range, don't force the pass; slow the tempo down and set up the offense in the halfcourt.

HOW TO ATTACK A ZONE DEFENSE

If your opponent plays a zone defense instead of man-to-man, there are certain basic things you have to do to keep the offense moving. These include (1) moving the ball quickly, (2) overloading (stationing more offensive players on one side of the court than defensive players), (3) isolating one defender against two offensive players. Against a zone, you need a good weak side offensive rebounder, and you need a center or forward who's a good shooter and ball-handler on the high post and can spot players open for shots and get the ball to them quickly.

DEVELOPING INDIVIDUAL OFFENSIVE MOVES

As I said earlier, most offensive plays break down before they are completed, so offense comes down to 1-on-1 or 2-on-2. In that situation, you have to know your effective shooting range and be able to get open for the right shot within that range, or get the ball to the player who is open.

Whether you're moving with or without the ball, you have to vary your patterns and moves. You can use fakes (head and shoulder, or step and crossover) to get into the clear when you're moving without the ball. When you have the ball, you fake to set up shots or passes. I don't want to give you specific fakes to work on because each player should develop his or her own moves. If you can dribble well (ideally with either hand), have a good change of pace, a crossover dribble, and a good first step off the dribble, you have the basic ingredients. Then you can add some seasoning: head and shoulder fakes, stutter steps, stop and go, that kind of thing.

The basic foundation of most fakes and moves is being able to pivot. Every player should be able to execute a single pivot, double pivot and reverse pivot. Pivot moves without the ball help you get open because you can get a step on the defender. Pivot moves with the ball, especially the reverse pivot, not only buy you a step but give you a foundation for both an outside shot and a drive to the basket. In order to reverse pivot properly, you should be able to dribble with both hands, and remember to keep sliding your front foot—the foot closest to the basket—ahead of the defensive player so he doesn't have a chance to step out and cut you off.

It's important not only to develop moves that work for you, but to avoid falling into predictable patterns. If you're guarded by an alert defensive player, he or she will quickly spot your patterns and react to them. You have to keep the defense guessing and off balance. For example, if you always dribble three times at half speed and then accelerate, or you always dribble twice prior to shooting, someone will spot those tendencies and know when to make a move to steal the ball.

Having said this, if you've developed a certain move or fake that works consistently, don't stop using it as long as it works; just mix it up with some other moves. And if you get beaten by the defense—the ball is stolen or your shot is blocked—you don't necessarily have to put that move in cold storage; figure out how to adjust so it works better. Maybe you need to execute faster, fake more convincingly, draw the defender closer first; maybe you're telegraphing what you're going to do.

LEARN YOUR TEAMMATES' MOVES AND SKILLS

You need to know your teammates' moves and skills as well as your own. That's what team play is about. Which of your teammates is going to beat his defender consistently, who has a good move to the basket from a certain point on the court, who can be counted on to screen for you, who needs help if he's challenged while dribbling, who will pick up your man on defense if he gets loose.

If you're able to execute certain moves well, i.e., a reverse pivot, you may draw double coverage. That means at least one of your teammates is open. Where? Can you get the ball to him? What type of pass will work best in that situation? At first you'll make up these things as you go along, but the longer you play with a team, the more you'll learn to anticipate each other's moves and act accordingly. In particular, when you play guard, it's important that you and the other guards get to know each other. Guard play requires quick passes, constant changes of speed and direction, good timing and being able to anticipate each other's moves.

You can develop all sorts of moves and fakes as an individual practicing on your own, or playing one-on-one, but any time you join forces with someone else at whatever level of competition, you have to integrate your game into a style that works best for your team so you can win together.

DAILY PRACTICE CHECKLIST

You'll need to work with other people to practice moving without the ball, setting picks, the pick and roll, or the fast break. You can run fast break passing drills and the pick and roll with just one or two teammates, although it's more beneficial to run them against defensive players. You can also practice shooting as you come off a screen. You can work on individual offensive moves and fakes all day long. If you don't have anyone with whom you can play one-on-one or two-on-two, do as I did. Set up chairs, stacks of books, any sort of marker, and practice your reverse pivots, crossover dribbles, change of pace, stutter steps and the like, moving toward or away from the markers. Concentrate on developing your quickness, flexibility, and ball control. Then apply what you've practiced whenever the opportunity arises for a pickup game.

OSCAR ROBERTSON CAREER HIGHLIGHTS

CRISPUS ATTUCKS HIGH SCHOOL

Started for three years, all except first game of sophomore season (freshmen not eligible). Scored 1780 points over three years, including 24.6 average senior year with a single game high of 62. Led Attucks to a 45-game winning streak over his last two seasons, including two consecutive Indiana state championships; scored a record 39 points in the 1956 finals. (Attucks was the first African-American school to win the Indiana state championship and the national championship, and the first school from Indianapolis to win the state title.) High school first team All-American. Named Indiana's "Mr. Basketball" in 1956. Member of the Indiana Basketball Hall of Fame.

UNIVERSITY OF CINCINNATI

Three-year starter (freshmen not eligible), co-captain junior and senior seasons. First player to lead NCAA in scoring three consecutive years with averages of 35.1, 32.6 and 33.7. Led University of Cincinnati to NCAA regionals in 1957 and Final Four in 1958 and 1959. Team compiled an overall three-year record of 79-9 (.897). Three-time unanimous All-American; numerous National Player of the Year honors all three seasons. Established 18 school, 16 Missouri Valley Conference and 14 NCAA scoring records. Team leader in scoring, rebounding, assists and free throw percentage. East-West All-Star Game, 1959 (Most Outstanding Player) and 1960; U.S. Pan-American team, 1959. Co-captain with Jerry West of 1960 undefeated Gold Medalist U.S. Olympic Basketball Team.

Career totals:

YEARS	GAMES	MIN	FG	FGA	PCT	FT	FTA	PCT	REB	AVG	AST	AVG	PF	PTS	AVG	W-L
1957-60	88	3412	1052	1968	.535	869	1114	.780	1338	15.2	425*	7.1*	---	2973	33.8	79-9

*assist statistics not kept during sophomore season

NATIONAL BASKETBALL ASSOCIATION

Cincinnati Royals, 1960-61—1969-70; Milwaukee Bucks, 1970-71—73-74. Rookie of the Year, 1961; Most Valuable Player, 1964 (first guard named MVP). Named to NBA All-Star team 12 consecutive seasons, 1960-61—1971-72; All-Star Game MVP, 1961, 1964, 1969. First player ever to average a "triple double," 1961-62, 30.8 points/game, 11.4 assists, 12.5 rebounds; averaged cumulative "triple double" first five seasons. Led NBA in free throw percentage, 1963-64, 1967-68; total career free throws; average assists eight of first nine seasons; all-time NBA assist leader with 9,887 and 9.5 per game until record broken by Magic Johnson in 1991. Led Cincinnati Royals to playoffs six consecutive years, 1961-62—1966-67, Milwaukee Bucks four straight years, 1970-71—1973-74; NBA championship, 1970-71. Elected President of National Basketball Players Association, 1963-1974. Named one of NBA's Top 50 Players of all time, 1997. Member, National Basketball Hall of Fame.

Career regular season totals:

YEARS	GAMES	MIN	FG	FGA	PCT	FT	FTA	PCT	REB	AVG	AST	AVG	PF	PTS	AVG	W-L
1960-74	1040	43866	9508	19620	.485	7694	9185	.838	7804	7.5	9887	9.5	2931	26710	25.7	685-465

Career Playoff totals

YEARS	GAMES	MIN	FG	FGA	PCT	FT	FTA	PCT	REB	AVG	AST	AVG	PF	PTS	AVG	W-L
62-67,71-74	86	3673	675	1456	.460	560	655	.855	578	6.7	769	8.9	267	1910	22.2	46-41

Career All-Star Game totals

YEARS	GAMES	MIN	FG	FGA	PCT	FT	FTA	PCT	REB	AVG	AST	AVG	PF	PTS	AVG	W-L
1961-72	12	380	88	172	.512	70	98	.714	69	5.8	61	5.1	41	246	20.5	11-1